Rehearsing THE MIDDLE SCHOOL ORCHESTRA

Sandy B. Goldie

Published by
Meredith Music Publications
a division of G.W. Music, Inc.
1584 Estuary Trail, Delray Beach, Florida 33483
http://www.meredithmusic.com

MEREDITH MUSIC PUBLICATIONS and its stylized double M logo are trademarks of
MEREDITH MUSIC PUBLICATIONS, a division of G.W. Music, Inc.

International Standard Book Number: 978-1-57463-498-3
Cataloging-in-Publication Data is on file with the Library of Congress.
Library of Congress Control Number: 2019938082
Printed and bound in U.S.A.

23 22 21 20 19 PP 1 2 3 4 5

Dedicated in loving memory of
Rebecca "Becky" Tyree

Contents

"When given the choice between sounding ugly or beautiful, choose the beautiful."

"As music educators, our role is to uncover and nurture each child's strengths through music. We must foster an identity within our students as lifelong music lovers regardless of performance strength."

"Teaching orchestra is my dream job. I cannot imagine doing anything else with my life." —Sarah

"I have the best job in the world because I can share my love and passion for music with my students." —Amy

"There are few greater privileges than touching the souls of middle school students while teaching them to make music on a string instrument."

"Never stop counting!

"Play with passion, precision, and unity. Make music, not notes."

"It took me a long time to come to the conclusion that talent is not what is important. Persistence, grit, and determination is what leads people to success over time."

Acknowledgments

This book represents an orchestra community's shared insights into teaching and rehearsing the middle school orchestra. I am grateful to each one of these contributors for taking the time and energy to share honestly, openly, and unguarded about their ideas and experiences working with middle school orchestras across the country. All too often, we orchestra teachers operate in isolation and some of the greatest ideas for working with middle school orchestras remain hidden behind the closed doors of the classroom or concert hall.

A heartfelt thank you to each of these educators. I am proud to call you my colleagues as we continue to work passionately together in the string music education profession:

Michael Alexander
Angela Ammerman
Sarah Black Ball
Don Brubaker
Amy Clement
Rebecca MacLeod
Seth Gamba
Anne Marie Patterson
Margaret Selby
Mimi Zweig

I would like to say a special thank you to my husband, Amos Goldie, for his loving support always and to my dear friend and colleague, Susanna Klein, for her excellent advice, invaluable feedback and constant cheerleading along the way.

Finally, I am thankful for my editor at Meredith Music Publications, Garwood Whaley. To Gar, I say a heartfelt thank you, not just for the opportunity to share this work and make it a reality, or for your amazing work editing and providing insight on the ideas, but for your kindness, patience and support as I worked through the final pages of this book during a very difficult time in my life. The loss of my dear friend and colleague, Rebeca Tyree, weighed heavily on my heart and mind while writing and her joyful and positive example of music teaching continues to remind me of the power of small individual acts of human kindness in teaching, the power of showing empathy and acceptance to each other, and the most important element of what we do as music educators—human connection to each other and to our students.

Introduction

The idea behind this book was to provide a forum for a select group of highly successful middle school orchestra teachers from across the country to share their ideas, approaches, and strategies for rehearsing the middle school orchestra. These music educators have honed their skills through years of experience in the field, have navigated a positive pathway through trial and error, and their resilient, passionate pursuit of musical excellence and human connection have shaped and inspired many young musicians.

In each chapter, we gain insight into the variety, authenticity, and uniqueness of each individual teacher's approach. Each author has been asked to respond the same set of prompts, covering topics such as rehearsal philosophy, rehearsal preparation, repertoire, warm-up strategies, tone, bow control, intonation, recruiting and others. In each set of responses, we gain honest glimpses into their classrooms as we peek around the often-closed doors behind which these teachers work.

As I have read the thoughts of my esteemed colleagues, I have become newly invigorated by the interesting ideas and insights they share and become increasingly excited to share them with you. As you turn the final pages, I hope you will be inspired to do what these teachers have done ... throw open wide the doors of your classroom and share the ideas, tips, tricks, and strategies you have discovered and seek the ideas of others. May we continue to engage deeply in conversations with each other about our most basic and most profound beliefs, values, and philosophies about what it is, what it means, and why it matters to be a string teacher today.

Michael Alexander

> "When given the choice between sounding ugly or beautiful, choose the beautiful."

Dr. Michael Alexander *joined the faculty of Baylor University in 2006 after twenty-two years of teaching high school and middle school orchestras in Houston, Texas. While at Stratford High School, the orchestra was twice named the Texas State Honor Orchestra. Dr. Alexander's duties at Baylor include supervising string student teachers, instruction in classroom string pedagogy, directing the Baylor String Project, and conducting the Baylor Campus Orchestra. He has been featured as clinician/conductor for conferences and student groups across the United States and abroad. Alexander is coauthor of the* Orchestra Expressions *series,* Expressive Techniques for Orchestra, *and* Expressive Sight-Reading for Orchestra. *His research interests are in the areas of string sight-reading, improvisation, pedagogy, and history. His research has been published in the* Journal of Research in Music Education, UPDATE: Applications of Research in Music Education, String Research Journal, ISAME Selected Papers, Texas Music Education Research, American String Teacher, *and* Southwestern Musician.

Rehearsal Philosophy

My rehearsal philosophy is based on the end goal in mind: I want to achieve the highest level of performance possible at *every* concert—not just at contests or festivals. If every concert is well prepared (no matter what the literature), a contest or festival should be no more difficult. Balance the difficulty

1

of your program so that easier pieces can feature tone development while more difficult pieces show technical prowess. Remember: Most of your audiences will not perceive difficulty level unless something is poorly played.

Rehearsal Preparation

This may seem obvious, but you must know the score before you can teach it. Students can spot lack of preparation on your part when they see confusion on the podium. I suggest thoroughly marking the score for pieces at every level and recommend a process outlined in the article "Fast and Efficient Ways to Prepare a Score" (available at https://www.tmea.org/resources/southwestern-musician/archive/article?swm_id=161).

With the end in mind, think backward from the concert date and plan time for each piece and the skills needed to play it. Break preparation down into weeks, then individual days. Prepare a rehearsal lesson plan for each week, and then, after listening to Friday's play-through recording, write your daily lesson plans and make modifications as necessary through the week. Even twenty-year veterans make lesson plans (even if it is on the back of their Starbucks cup on the way to work!). If your students do not play well in third position or don't have a great spiccato, don't program pieces that require those techniques yet. Instead, use the warm-up to develop those skills that the students will need on the *next* concert.

Warm-up

Dr. Anne Witt calls the orchestral warm-up "teaching time." I fully agree that the warm-up—not the rehearsal—is the place to teach, practice, and refine new skills. If we try to teach skills through literature in rehearsal, the literature becomes bogged down in technical study and we can drill the life out of it. That being said, rehearsal becomes the place we *apply* techniques previously taught in the warm-up. My advice is never to program a piece unless you have presented and practiced the required techniques in your warm-up many times before.

Intonation and Fluency: Developing the Left Hand

Review a finger pattern drill daily. If you do not already use one, see the opening exercises in *Daily Warm-up for Strings* by Michael Allen or *Expressive Technique for Orchestra* by Brungard, Alexander, Anderson, and Dackow. Also, teach a one-octave D chromatic scale by the end of the first year using both ascending and descending finger patterns. This will arm students with all the extensions needed to play in any key in first position and should get them through a good bit of the middle school literature. This is *much* easier than trying to teach isolated extensions occurring in your repertoire. Use a unison method for teaching shifting and positions.

Most importantly, involve students in the tuning process from the first day. Use electronic tuners to teach them how and how far to turn the fine tuners, and incorporate both individual and group tuning procedures. For more specific advice on the teaching of tuning in middle school ensembles, see "20 Ways to Get Your String Orchestra to Play in Tune" (available at https://www.tmea.org/assets/pdf/southwestern_musician/20WaystoTune_Sept2012.pdf). See also "Teaching Tuning to the String Orchestra: Classroom Procedures for Beginning to Advanced Students" (*American String Teacher*, 58 (4), 20–26).

Tone: Developing the Right Hand and Bow Control

Four factors determine production of a good tone: bow speed, bow weight, bow placement, and part of the bow. While bow placement (between the bridge and the fingerboard) is used primarily for dynamic contrast, bow weight and bow speed must be balanced to create a good tone in any part of the bow (frog, middle, tip). Dr. Sandra Dackow uses the term "traction" to describe the ideal balance of bow weight and bow speed. I love this term in that it implies that the bow should not skim over the string or crunch into the string. Rather, appropriate traction results in a full, rich tone. Have students experiment with tone production at various dynamics and in different parts of the bow during your warm-up time. Once a variety of bow placements can be played at various dynamics with a good tone, these can be transferred to the literature.

I recommend teaching bowing styles and articulations through the use of a programmed warm-up, such as those found in *Daily Warm-up for Strings* by Michael Allen or *Expressive Technique for Orchestra* by Brungard, Alexander, Anderson, and Dackow. Teach one new section each week until the entire warm-up is learned. Michael Allen likened the use of such warm-ups to taking your daily multivitamins: You may not need all the techniques for any particular piece or rehearsal, but the daily practice of a variety of styles prepares you for *every* piece.

To build a relaxed bow hold and flexible wrist, encourage students to "wax on/wax off" without the bow in their hand. Encourage students to practice Galamian's "flexive and reflexive" fingers with a pencil bow hold while they are sitting with their arm supported by a desk. (It will drive their math teachers nuts!)

Set-up/Fundamentals: Instrument Position and Body Alignment
Most modern method books have photos or line drawings that illustrate appropriate proper instrument position and body alignment. Use these, and make sure that students *and* parents refer to them during home practice. My favorite phrase for cello and bass players is, "Sit tall." For violin and viola, I like the Suzuki School mantra: "Is my scroll as high as my nose? Is my elbow over my toes?"

Ensemble Playing: Unity, Precision, Tempo Stability
I was amazed the first time I saw Denese Odegaard present a clinic on unifying a string section. While most of us add one player at a time to the principal player, she matches each individual player to the principal to establish individual responsibility for matching the section leader. The difference in the two approaches is that the first hides the sound of players in the back of the section while the second combines the individual players into a unified sound. It may take a little longer, but the difference is astounding!

When a group is rushing, I have found success in stabilizing a tempo by providing a metronomic pulse on the subdivision of the beat or by clapping the back-beats (beats 2 and 4) while they are playing.

When students are playing imprecise rhythms, I often have them play the passage pizzicato. It makes the imprecise notes *very* obvious, and students will quickly work to unify their sound, as no one wants to be the outlier.

Expression: Phrasing, Balance, Dynamic Contrast
"The most beautiful distance between two points is a curved line." Dr. B. R. Henson's quote has shaped my musicality since graduate school. I

have found that if phrases can be achieved, intonation and rhythm follow naturally. I often have students mark the top of a phrases with an asterisk so they know where they are headed.

Articulation Control
Work on unifying articulation concepts as an ensemble during the warm-up time. Use a unison programmed warm-up to teach concepts, and review them on a regular basis. In rehearsal, clearly define the style desired with a student example, then match players using Denese Odegaard's method described earlier to build a unified approach to the articulation desired.

Repertoire
Select repertoire that showcases the skills that you have already taught. Remember: The new skills you are introducing during warm-ups should be in preparation for the *next* set of repertoire. Select a variety of pieces, some for beautiful tone and others for flashy technique. Kids like pieces that are high, fast, and loud, so those are easy choices. More difficult are the slower but beautiful pieces in the repertoire. If you bring out the phrasing on a slower yet well-written piece, it is often the audience favorite. I call it the "make yo' momma cry" piece, and every program needs one. Some of my favorites are:

- "M to the Third Power," by Carold Nunez
- "Modal Festival," by Jon Marsh
- "Can Can," by Jacques Offenbac/arr. Merle J. Isaac
- "Ukranian Folk Song Suite," arr. Sandra Dackow
- "Cello Rondo," by M.L. Daniels

Recruiting/Community Building
The best recruiting tools you have are your current students and parents. If they are excited about the program, they will encourage their friends and neighbors. Be a good teacher, and they will come. During sign-up time, I asked current students to bring me the names of three new students they had recruited from their neighborhood. Combined with the usual recruitment concerts and other traditional techniques, this worked like a charm.

Angela Ammerman

> "As music educators, our role is to uncover and nurture each child's strengths through music. We must foster an identity within our students as lifelong music lovers regardless of performance strength."

Angela Ammerman *is the Coordinator and Assistant Professor of Music Education at the University of Tennessee at Martin, where she also directs the orchestra. Dr. Ammerman holds degrees from the University of Cincinnati: College-Conservatory of Music and Boston University, and was awarded the very first PhD in Music Education from George Mason University. Dr. Ammerman has been featured in the* Washington Post *for her innovative and energetic teaching style and has been referred to as the first "music teacher prodigy." Recognized by the Virginia House of Delegates for her dedication to instilling a lifelong passion for music in all of her students, Angela Ammerman diligently works to now pass along these teaching and mentorship qualities to her own music education students. Dr. Ammerman has been named the Virginia Orchestra Director of the Year, has been a finalist for Fairfax County Public Schools' Teacher of the Year, and has been recognized as FCPS' Top Teacher. Dr. Ammerman is in high demand as a guest conductor and clinician and is known for her emphasis on play-based learning and humor, and for the creation of the first-ever Future Music Educators Camp, as well as for her music education podcast, #MusicEdLove.*

Rehearsal Philosophy

The benefits of music and music education are many, but one of the greatest benefits is the innately social act of coming together to achieve something larger than one might achieve alone. In 2014, researchers found that musicians engaged in exertive rhythmic activities experienced a spike in endorphins (also known as the "happy" chemical) (Tarr, Launay, and Dunbar). Additionally, student decisions on whether or not to continue in strings are directly linked to the individual's perception of social status within the orchestra (Ammerman and Wuttke, 2014). If an ultimate goal is to build in our students a lifelong love of music, then we must form social connections between musicians so that music becomes not only a class students take but a life that they live. We must bring in a variety of repertoire that allows students to gain insight and appreciation for music from other cultures and encourages students to seek out new musical experiences. Finally, we must make musicking so enjoyable that students want to return to our classes and become intrinsically motivated to learn and to improve, so that once they graduate from our programs, they continue to crave the satisfaction gained from a fruitful rehearsal.

The goals of the successful rehearsal are to:

- spark happy feelings in our young musicians by encouraging group participation in exertive rhythmic and tonal activities
- build in all of our musicians a sense of social belonging and cultural acceptance so that they experience music making as a cohesive unit
- foster in our students the drive to seek out and experience higher level processing and performing through sequential successes in learning and performing within our own classrooms

Rehearsal Preparation

Among the most important considerations for preparing a prosperous rehearsal are the acts of listening, musical work research, and score study. You have selected your repertoire (hopefully by listening and checking out scores), and now it's time to plan your lessons. Consider assigning listening projects to students in which they must listen along with their sheet music. Ask specific questions that address moments in the music. If the piece notates *col legno* but you haven't yet addressed this in class, have students identify the exact moment all of the musicians turn their bows to use the stick! In addition to listening to recordings, students might also do a little bit of composer and musical work research so that everyone is prepared to discuss important and relevant aspects of the piece as needed. Finally, search the entire score for the three different types of passages: Morale Boosters, Technical Traps, and Musicality Mazes. See the chart on the following page for more information about these and to gain insight into a highly successful method for planning for your rehearsal.

Warm-Up

Before we get to the warm-up itself, let us discuss what happens before the warm-up. We must never underestimate the power of the initial greeting at the beginning of class. A teacher waiting for students with a smile and a song is like the sun coming up at the start of each and every class. Consider creative ways to greet your musicians in order to best spark interest in your lesson. My dream teaching environment involves music pouring out of the classroom, seeping into the ears of all of the passersby, enticing the outside world to join in, excitement bubbling out, piquing the interest of humans from all backgrounds, calling them inside, into a land of acceptance, love, and growth.

Here are just a few hooks you can use to reel in not only your students but even non-string students, faculty members, and staff.

Rhythmic Masterminds
1. Draw a moderately tricky rhythm on a sheet of paper.
2. As students walk in, they must tap, stomp, or "boogie" that rhythm.
3. Have some kind of a musical accompaniment blaring from within the classroom so the players can keep time!

Composer Quote
1. Play music from a composer of your choice on speakers in your classroom.
2. Write out a quote from this composer on a big sheet of paper.
3. Students must read it aloud in either a different accent or with dramatic flair before walking in.
   ***Warning!** This one is a huge hit with middle school students and often gets non-string people involved!

The Ammermanian Guide to Rehearsal Success

CHARACTERISTICS OF PASSAGE	PROCESS	HELPFUL HINTS*
Morale Boosters		

Morale Boosters contain:
• limited or no shifting
• simple finger patterns
  ○ limited accidentals
  ○ rhythmic simplicity
  ○ quarter notes
  ○ half notes
  ○ whole notes
  ○ some repeated eighth notes
Musicians will:
• be fairly successful the first or second time they read these passages
• be able to quickly add another dimension into the performance (dynamic contrast, phrasing, etc.)
• feel confident and prepared to move into more challenging sections after performing these
	1. Start and end with Morale Boosters.
	2. Praise students for successes here (they may not experience the same kind of success in other moments in class).
	3. Allow students to play through longer passages of music during this section so that they experience a broader view of the music.
	
	EXTENSION:
	If students are successful during these sections, work to prepare students for the Musical Mazes here by encouraging musical elements such as:
	  a. vibrato
	  b. phrasing
	  c. eye contact with other sections
		Placement:
		Beginning and end of class
		Time Allocation:
		< 20% of class
		Hints:
		Working on these passages will boost morale in your classroom and can be enough for students to look forward to returning for future classes, even if the middle of the class was extremely challenging. We always want our students to look forward to returning to our class!

Technicality Traps		

Technicality Traps contain:
• moderate-to-extensive shifting
• complex finger patterns
• accidentals
• rhythmic complexity
  ○ syncopation
  ○ alternating/ moving eighth or sixteenth notes
  ○ tricky entrances
Musicians will:
• experience difficulty and frustration the first or second (or beyond) time they read these passages
• need extra time and instruction
• feel hugely successful after mastering just one technicality trap and may feel encouraged to continue to the next
	1. Break rehearsals into manageable chunks (2–4 measures at a time)
	2. Prepare multiple additional teaching methods ahead of time.
	  a. Write lyrics to the passage, and have the students sing them out loud.
	  b. Create technique exercises that match the technicality trap.
	  c. Practice until the scales are balanced out so that students are now more likely to succeed than to fail.
	
	EXTENSION:
	For students who may experience success quicker than others, have them create tutorials (video, audio, or even warm-ups) for the class!
		Placement:
		Second part of class, immediately after Morale Boosters
		Time Allocation:
		< 35% of class
		Hints
		These passages can sometimes be frustrating for students. Musicians will learn best toward the beginning of class after they are warmed up and have experienced heightened self-confidence thanks to the Morale Boosters.

9

continues

CHARACTERISTICS OF PASSAGE	PROCESS	HELPFUL HINTS*
Musicality Mazes		

Musical Mazes contain:
• intense passages
• dissonances
• mature thematic and/or storyline material (death, heartbreak, love, etc.)
• strong emotive elements
• limited written dynamics
Musicians may:
• experience success in playing only the written notes and rhythms at first
• struggle to understand that more is needed to communicate with an audience than what is written
• identify strongly with the material once they understand the storyline and/or emotive elements of the passage
	1. Play through the passage as written on the page.
	2. Listen to recordings of professionals playing these passages. Ask students to identify what was played that was not present on the page.
	3. Discuss ways to expand the musical material (dynamics, phrasing, etc.).
	  a. Try out different musical ideas.
	  b. Ask students which musical ideas they prefer and why.
	  c. Vote on an appropriate musical expansion.
	
	EXTENSION:
	Consider bringing in additional materials to provide further understanding of passages. Materials might include:
	  a. artwork from this time period
	  b. composer memoirs, letters, biographies, etc.
	  c. poetry that connects with the piece
		Placement:
		Third part of class, immediately after Technicality Traps
		Time Allocation:
		< 30% of class
		Hints:
		These are sometimes the most challenging passages for young musicians due to the emotional maturity required. Remember to work toward a safe environment in which students are never made to feel less valued than others. Encourage expression, and make emoting seem like something acceptable and cool even!

Note that the time allocation percentages do not add up to 100%. Although orchestra is primarily a performance class, we must remember to include activities that are not purely performance-based, including composition, improvisation, history, and theory.

Tricky Time

1. Prepare a short excerpt of music in which one measure has too many notes for the time signature.
2. In order to enter the room, students must identify the wrong measure and tell you how to fix it.

Once you have reeled your students in, it is time to get to the warm-up. Consider composing your own warm-ups to specifically address problem spots within the music, standards in your lesson, and overarching techniques you are hoping to resolve over the school year. See below for warm-up options.

Warm-Ups for an Efficient Ensemble Rehearsal

CATEGORY	PREP TIME REQUIRED	PREPARATION/PROCESS

Variations on Rehearsal Pieces	Significant (30–60 minutes)	1. Select 4–5 challenging passages within piece.
		2. For each passage, compose a homogenous warm-up in which the notes and rhythms are:
		  ○ rhythmically augmented (turn the eighth notes into quarter notes, etc.)
		  ○ doubled/tripled
		  ○ repeated for 3–4 measures with variations
		  ○ played down or up an octave
		  ○ sung!
		3. Give it a silly title so students will look forward to getting it out. For example, "The Decomposing Composer." (Middle schoolers love this kind of humor.)

Tone Quality	Moderate (10–30 minutes)	1. Select one chord progression.
		2. Write out the notes for each chord so that students can easily identify them.
		3. Have students play the tones slowly with the most beautiful tone possible as you walk around to adjust bow position and weight.
		4. Once musicians are achieving a characteristic tone, encourage one section at a time to find a corner. Ask them to:
		  a. face into the corner with instrument
		  b. play their note, listening only to themselves
		  c. test out a variety of bow weights and placements until they are happy with their tone quality
		(Make sure all students are playing the entire time, even if only one section is moving to a corner.)

Aural Skills	Minimal (2–10 minutes)	1. Select intervals/passages for which students are struggling. 2. You play; they repeat. 3. Continue the process. 4. Begin to switch up the intervals, adding accidentals and/or new note lengths. 5. Try playing one note out of tune to see if students can identify the problem pitch.
Exercises from the Book	Minimal (2–10 minutes)	1. Select tricky passages. 2. Identify scalar/rhythmic patterns within passage. 3. Search "the book" for exercises that will support these passages. 4. Work through the exercises, then immediately delve into those tricky passages. 5. Jump back and forth between the piece and the warm-ups as much as is helpful.

11

Intonation and Fluency: Developing the Left Hand

Many students struggle with knowing whether or not they are playing in tune, especially in a large ensemble. It is necessary to start ear training exercises as early as possible. Here are just a few ways to improve student aural skills:

- Daily listening assignments
- Daily singing exercises
- "Dr. ViolINTune" exercises. For these, students must:
  - Diagnose the problem.
  - Prescribe a "treatment."
  - Assess the patient after treatment to determine whether or not the patient was healed.

Use these exercises throughout the year to encourage positive aural growth. In addition to ear training activities, consider providing a visual element to aid those students with poor intonation. Use tapes at the beginning for students who may struggle with hearing intervals. Finally, work to achieve precise finger placement by practicing the various "Star Trek" String Greetings, which include the various finger patterns required of your group.

Once your students have mastered their first-position finger patterns, it may be time to teach shifting. Even when doing simple shifting exercises, it might be helpful to have some kind of a D major pop song playing in the background. Even our exercises can be mindfully musical! I have found that a sequential approach to shifting is quite successful. Try the exercise below to get students started with shifting while maintaining focus on left-hand position and sound:

1. Play G on the D string in first position.
2. Slide into G on the D string.
3. Continue to practice the back-and-forth between third position and first position.
4. Then, practice a silent slide.
   a. Play G on the D string in first position.
   b. Silent slide.
   c. Play G on the D string in third position.
   d. Once they can get the placement right, switch to playing a D on the A string, and repeat the process.

As you work on extensions, shifting, and appropriate finger patterns, try having students play songs that are familiar to them in unusual positions. This is a great way to aid ear training while still working on the objective in an enjoyable way. And remember to ask musicians to take their thumbs with them as they slide and to encourage a reliance on listening rather than visual placement.

Tone: Developing the Right Hand and Bow Control
Teaching tone can be an incredibly challenging task, particularly if students do not have the highest quality of instruments. It is important to ensure, first and foremost, that students have a quality bow hold. When teaching bow hold, work to encourage flexibility from the beginning. Have students practice lifting different fingers on the bow to see if they can maintain flexibility. Use a more legato tone in your voice even when discussing bow hold. I love to teach bow hold and placement with the lights off and a gentle drone in the background. Start with exercises that focus primarily on setting the bow in the sweet spot and lifting it back up so that students can continue to work on the bow hold. Throughout all of the bowing exercises, encourage students to maintain a relaxed and loose right hand.

As students begin to advance in tone production, encourage movement at an early stage. Work to get students to use opposing motion with their bow, particularly in slower passages. On a down-bow, have students move into a more open position so that their body moves slightly away from the bow. On an up-bow, students move into more of a closed position in which the bow and instrument are quite close. This allows students to get the most sound out of their bow and to mimic—at first—the physical process of emoting. Teaching students how to move when they play is an essential component of tone development and performance technique and allows students to embody musical passages once they feel compelled.

Set-Up/Fundamentals: Instrument Position and Body Alignment
Setting up the student-musician is one of the most important aspects of the job of an orchestra director. We must take great care to set up students properly while still making learning enjoyable. As we teach instrument set-up, have a bit of fun. As students master the appropriate set-up, work

to document their progress. Take before and after selfies of their postures, for example!

Setting up the Instrument: The 1-2-3, Play-for-Me Cadence
(Students should be standing for this, cellists and basses with endpin extended.)

VIOLIN/VIOLA	
Teacher calls cadence style, students repeat:	**Teacher Actions**
"One! Two!"	1. Stomp left foot. 2. Stomp right foot.
"Three! Four!"	3. Hold instrument out in front of you by the neck. 4. Set right hand on butt of instrument.
"Five is the flip."	5. Turn instrument upside down vertically. (Scroll should be pointed toward the ground.)
"Six. Lay down!"	6. Lay instrument flat on forearm.
"Seven is the Slide!"	7. Slide instrument up into position on shoulder.
"Eight for the Eyes!"	8. Turn head toward scroll and set down.
"Nine. Check your Wrist!"	9. Move wrist in and then out into appropriate posture. (Use right hand fingers to push wrist back out.)
"Ten is the Wiggle!"	10. Wiggle elbow, tap thumb, wiggle fingers.

CELLO/BASS	
Teacher calls cadence style, students repeat:	**Teacher Actions**
"One! Two!"	1. Stomp left foot. 2. Stomp right foot.
"Three! Four!"	3. Hold instrument out in front of you by the neck. 4. Sit on edge of chair.
"Five is the skip."	5. Shuffle both feet up and then back down.
"Six. Lay down!"	6. Pull instrument close to body.
"Seven is the Slide!"	7. Slide left hand into place with elbow up.
"Eight for the Ears!"	8. Nod head for cellists to show the C peg connection to the left ear.
"Nine. Check the Thumb Love!"	9. Tap middle finger and thumb together away from instrument, then move to instrument and tap on fingerboard.
"Ten is the Wiggle!"	10. Wiggle elbow, tap thumb, wiggle fingers.

14

Ensemble Playing: Unity, Precision, Tempo Stability

When rehearsing our ensembles, we must encourage synchronicity in every way possible. Encourage musicians to:

- Breathe together before important entrances.
- Make eye contact with other sections.
- Fully understand who has the part that coincides with their own.

In addition, you may want to:

- Rehearse passages with a drone in the background in the same key as your piece; this will fill students' ears with the tonic.
- Set your metronome to the "beatbox" in order to achieve a steady tempo but also in order to have an unusual and relatable experience within your class.
- Record rehearsals, and play them back so students can hear what the ensemble as a whole really sounds like.

The more experiences you can create where students are making music, having fun, and experiencing growth, the better off your program will be!

Expression: Phrasing, Balance, Dynamic Contrast

Teaching expression within the middle school orchestra can be uniquely challenging. Students are experiencing overwhelming physical changes and may be reluctant to emote during class. Turn expressive passages into games until students become comfortable.

In order to improve balance and listening within the ensemble, have the students do a "Pineapple Upside Down Cake" where students:

1. move anywhere within the room (outside of their own section and without their stand partner)
2. play passages and listen to how their part works with others around them
3. return to their seats while keeping in mind the practice of listening for the parts they just heard

Movement exercises are also helpful to improving expression. Try the following activities to aid expression:

- Ask your musicians to slowly stand through a crescendo, then to sit back down through a decrescendo.

- Take suggestions from your students for characters and plot lines for the piece of music you are rehearsing. Ask students to embody this story musically and physically.
- Write lyrics for musical passages, and have contests to see who can sing or play the passage with the most appropriate expression.

Articulation Control

Articulation control can be a challenging topic within the middle school orchestra. Make these activities enjoyable and bring in some "puppy love."

- Spiccato is the bouncing puppy, loose and buoyant. He jumps from just the right height or else he bounces out of control.
- Accent is the dog in desperate need of some serious training. He bites and pulls on his leash, and he barks louder than everyone else.
- Legato is trained for shows. Her gait is so smooth that you can't even tell when she changes directions.

Although it may seem silly, my students especially enjoy these stories if I bring in goofy pictures of dogs in ribbons and hats.

2.2 Legato (2014). Westminster Kennel Club Dog Show.
Licensed under creative commons on wikimediacommons.com

2.3 Accent (1957). Florida Memory. Licensed under creative commons on flickr.com

Figure 3. Spiccato. Way, Emery. (2009). "No Strings."
Licensed under creative commons on flickr.com

Repertoire

When selecting repertoire, I recommend three factors to help you make your decisions:

- **Student Cultural Background.** Select at least some music that represents the cultures of your students. This shows the students and families that you respect and appreciate their backgrounds.
- **Standards to Work On.** As the guides to our students' musical journeys, we want to ensure that they get an appropriate amount of material from various time periods, cultures, and styles.
- **Spiciness Scale.** Think of your musical selection as a healthy balance of spice! I like to have at least one of the following in each program:

For example, here is a list of pieces I have greatly enjoyed working on with middle school orchestras:

The B.P.G. Scale of Spice		
PREDICTIONS	**CHARACTERISTICS**	**SPICINESS LEVEL**
Guaranteed Success Select one or two.	Not easy, necessarily, but just barely above students' present level.	Bell Pepper
The Moderate Challenge Select one or two.	These pieces include technical traps and musicality mazes that may confuse students. These pieces require that the students focus in class and do an acceptable amount of practicing.	Poblano Pepper
The Extreme Challenge Select no more than one, depending on the skill of your ensemble.	These pieces often require a significant amount of practice time outside of class and may not always be stellar at concert time. *Excellent for advanced groups who are willing to put in the work and time.*	Ghost Pepper

TITLE	COMPOSER/ ARRANGER	SPICINESS LEVEL FOR A TYPICAL SEVENTH-/EIGHTH- GRADE ORCHESTRA
Anasazi	Edmondson	Bell Pepper
Korean Folk Tune	Arr. Meyer	Bell Pepper
Las Mariposas Exoticas	Spata	Bell Pepper
Escape from Black Licorice Forest	Frueh	Poblano Pepper
Ghost Ship	Arr. Story	Poblano Pepper
Pavanne for a Dead Princess	Ravel/Olah	Poblano Pepper
Two South American Tangos	Villoldo	Poblano Pepper
Bartok Folk Trilogy	Arr. McGinty	Ghost Pepper
Hungarian Dance No. 5	Brahms/Isaac	Ghost Pepper
Russian Sailors Dance	Gliere/Allen	Ghost Pepper

19

Recruiting

SEVEN Ps OF MARKETING	STRING ORCHESTRA RECRUITING CONSTRUCTS	STRING ORCHESTRA EQUIVALENT
Product/Place	Program	A string program in its entirety (initial enrollment to grade 12)
Price	Subsidy	The financial requirements for a student to join
People	Outer Rewards	Branding giveaways— everything with your unique logo on it t-shirts pencils bumper stickers
Process	Communication	Rapport built between the director and the incoming students through recruiting concerts and special guest visits
Proof	Assessment	Rehearsals and interactions with potential students to demonstrate the enjoyable nature of working with the director
Promotion	Image	A successful and reputable program is a strong promotion in and of itself.

*Adapted from Kerstetter's Band Recruiting Construct

Recruiting/Community Building

There exists within the United States a shortage of string players, string programs, and string teachers. We must work to remedy this through the recruiting of musicians and the building of advocacy throughout our community. Here are just a few tips for recruiting and community building:

- Bring the "cool" factor.
  - Allow musicians to wear war paint for recruiting concerts.
  - Sign autographs afterwards!
- Present a variety of repertoire from pop to classical to even punk or hip-hop.

- Present options for students who may not speak English or who may not have the income to afford participation in your ensemble.
- Perform everywhere you can.
- Send your students to elementary schools as ambassadors.
- Send invitations to younger grades or to non-music classes for students to join your program and to attend your concerts.
- Post everything on social media.
- Get the local news stations to your events as often as possible.

Recruiting may sometimes feel as if it is an unwieldy project. Check out the table below for a research-based, systematic approach to recruiting throughout the year (Ammerman, 2017; Kerstetter, 2011). Address each of the seven Ps of marketing with targeted activities.

More importantly than all of this, however, is to remember to find some kind of greatness in each and every child (whether it is a musical greatness or not) so that all of your musicians know that they are welcomed, valued, and appreciated in your program. This is truly the best way to build your program.

Sarah Black Ball
and Amy Clement

"Teaching orchestra is my dream job. I cannot imagine doing anything else with my life."
—Sarah

"I have the best job in the world because I can share my love and passion for music with my students." —Amy

Sarah Black Ball *has been teaching orchestra for twenty-one years, all in Gwinnett County, Georgia. She is one of three orchestra teachers at North Gwinnett Middle School in Sugar Hill, Georgia.* **Amy Clement** *has been teaching orchestra for twenty-two years. She is also one of the three orchestra teachers at North Gwinnett Middle School.* **Amy and Sarah** *have team-taught together for thirteen years and would like to make this disclaimer: Most—if not all—of the ideas we are presenting have been borrowed from hundreds of colleagues. If you recognize something as your idea, thank you!*

Rehearsal Philosophy
We approach rehearsal from a realistic point of view. We assume that the only time students are playing their instruments is during class. How do we hold students accountable without practice records? Frequent playing tests (not necessarily seating tests) and rotational seating. Each student has a number that remains the same, but where that number is located can change. (They do travel with their stand partners to keep some security.) We also hold our students to high standards and do not accept bad posture, disruptive behavior, or bad intonation. Students will rise to whatever level you demand of them; how low or high you place the bar is up to you.

We keep the pacing fairly quick and try to keep all students engaged by assigning them a task to complete while we are working with other sections. We also incorporate games to keep rehearsal positive and fun. (A happy brain learns better.) One of our favorite go-to games is rehearsal tic-tac-toe.

1. Draw a giant tic-tac-toe board on your white board.
2. Allow the class to choose if they are X or O. (They usually pick X, so then the music would be O.)
3. Pick a passage of music. If students play it to your expectation, they get to put an X where they all agree upon. If not, the music gets to place an O.

This is an easy game and gets students very engaged in trying to win.

Rehearsal Preparation
We suggest deciding first what you want to teach or reinforce during a lesson. Before bringing it to your students, listen to the piece with the score in hand, then play through each part on the instrument that is assigned to that part. The process will immediately show you what spots will be tricky and where mistakes are likely to be made. Knowing this ahead of time allows you to prepare warm-ups and technique exercises that can be used to alleviate an issue before it even happens.

After you rehearse a section of music, you should reflect on what went well and what didn't as soon as possible so that you can create a new plan of attack. Do not fall into the trap of only rehearsing from the beginning of the music. Start in different places, and rehearse with a specific goal in mind. Obviously, fix anything blatantly wrong, but if your main objective for the day is to work on bowing or precision, don't spend a third of your class time working on dynamic contrast.

Warm-Up

Our favorite way to start a class is with simple "I play, you play" patterns. We teach very large classes, and it only takes our students a day or two to learn that as soon as they hear the teacher (or a classmate) playing a pattern on the podium, they ought to be prepared to play it back. This activity get them settled, focused, and ready to start very quickly, and it also gives students a chance to listen to the tuning of their instruments.

After a short series of open-string call-and-responses, we play four times on each open string. Students raise their hands if they need help tuning their instruments. Again, this puts the responsibility on the students to determine if they are in tune or not.

We also use warm-ups of call-and-response before every piece, not just at the beginning of class. It sets the basic finger patterns for that piece and allows us to isolate some tricky rhythms without having to read them first. Students can play almost anything they hear long before they see it. It is fun to play a tricky rhythm in a call-and-response format and then have students look at that same rhythm in their music without telling them it is identical. After much murmuring about how that looks "too hard," let them in on the secret that they all just performed it successfully. After they have heard it, played it successfully, and seen it on the page, they will understand it on a much deeper level.

Try to introduce a new, difficult technique or key signature outside of the repertoire a couple of weeks ahead of introducing the pieces so that when students see it in their sheet music, they are ready for it. On the other hand, try not to introduce complex concepts that will not relate to any upcoming pieces. For example, scales are fundamental, but it is important to have students apply the scales they are learning into their repertoire. Don't teach sixth-grade students a B-flat major scale if they aren't going to play anything in that key until the end of seventh grade.

Intonation and Fluency: Developing the Left Hand

The most important point to make to students about intonation is that there is no such thing as "close." It is either right or wrong. It is either in tune or out of tune. It is so important to establish high expectations from the beginning with your students and to insist that your students play in tune. Of course, eighth graders sound more in tune than beginners, but one could argue that that has much less to do with the left hand than it does with the right hand. A few things that seem to help our students with intonation are:

- Good left- and right-hand position.
- A lot of "I play, you play" so that they are constantly hearing good intonation modeled for them.
- Tuning chords from bottom to top and making sure students understand each note's function within a chord.
- Working on inner-voice intonation: tune the third, tune the third, tune the third!
- Helping students find the notes that make their open strings resonate. We even let them wear dollar-store rings on their third (violin/viola), fourth (cello), or first (bass) fingers to remind them that those fingers often have one of the ringing tones.
- Finger pattern charts that allow them to see different whole- and half-step patterns in different keys.
- Making sure half steps are close enough. We like to have students (violin/viola) try to hold a $20 bill between the index and middle finger of their left hand. If we can't grab it from them, they get to keep it. Make sure their fingers are straight and that they aren't grabbing with thumb or other fingers to add strength, and you should be able to nab the bill pretty easily. Even though they didn't make any money, show them that they have a perfect half-step (since fingers are touching), and remind them that that is something money can't buy.
- Using a tuner with projected drone over the group, or having other sections hold tonic or note that goes with the section you are working with. This helps with intonation and student engagement.
- Strong left hands. We do an activity early on in our beginning classes that allows students to squish a marshmallow between a

finger on their left hand and their thumb. We use the phrase "sink into the marshmallow," and then transfer that to the fingerboard and say, "Sink into the fingerboard." Even years later, we can simply say "marshmallow fingers," and that reminds them to sink in. Another phrase we use for the same concept is that "the left hand is always forte."

Tone: Developing the Right Hand and Bow Control

As stated earlier, we believe that tone is the biggest indication of a group's maturity level. It impacts everything from the core sound of the group to intonation. Correct right-hand position is a huge part of that. It is important to set up a relaxed, comfortable bow hold, and it is one of our favorite things to teach. First and foremost, repeat this to yourself: "Every day is bow-hold day!" Bow hold is probably one of the most important skills to reinforce early and often from day 1 to graduation and beyond. The bad news is that it could get pretty tedious really quickly. The awesome news is there are tons of bow-hold games and manipulatives at our disposal, and kids love them. Here are a few:

- **Bow Seatbelts.** This one is hard to describe in writing, but if you do an online search, you will find videos on how to do this on the bow. It will help students keep their middle and/or ring fingers over the frog. It prevents those two fingers from creeping up on top of the stick.
- **Straws.** We have a set of giant (36-inch) straws that work great, but regular straws work too. The reason I like setting up the bow hold on straws is that students can see if and where they are squeezing.
- **Spaghetti Noodles (uncooked).** This is the ninja level of not squeezing the bow. Obviously, if students hold with too much tension, the noodles break.
- **Pixie Stix.** This is the same idea as spaghetti or straws, though it only works if your school allows candy.
- **Glow Sticks.** Take a trip to your local dollar store (aka the teacher's best friend), and buy enough tubes of sticks to hand out to all of your students. Orchestra class doesn't get much cooler than when your students all build fabulous bow holds on glow sticks, turn out the lights, and then perform different motions in the air.

- **Spider Crawl.** This is a pretty common one. Students keep a good bow hold while their bow hands crawls up and down the stick of the bow. If you want to take this to the next level of fun, buy spider rings on clearance at Halloween and allow each student to wear a spider on their bow hand as it crawls up the stick of the bow.
- **Bow-Hold Parade.** Confession time, this is one of our favorites! Map out a parade route ahead of time. Tell students the parade route, have them set up their best bow hold, put on a great march (we use "Stars and Stripes Forever"), and let the parade begin. Explain to students that you will award particularly fabulous bow holds with a prize (candy, stickers, choice of seat, lead warm-ups, etc.). You will be amazed at how much attention they pay to the details when a Jolly Rancher is at stake.
- **Bow-lympics.** Once you have a repertoire of at least seven or eight games, you can have Bow-lympics day. This works great after a concert, on a day when many of your kids are gone on a field trip, or on one of those last days of school. Set up stations around the room or in the hallway and assign students all kinds of bow-hold tasks. You can make it a competition or more of a casual bow-hold field day! Alternate name: Bow-nanza.
- **Pirate Story.** This is how we first introduce the bow hold. We tell students a story with pirates so they can remember each finger has a place and function. The thumb is the captain with his bumpy chin (bent) and he hates bananas. The two middle fingers are pirates that dangle their feet in the water. The index finger is the sleepy, lazy pirate laying down on the job, and violin/viola pinkies are scared of the water, so they are on top of the stick. Cello/bass pinky pirates like to dangle their feet in the water too. Here is the most important fact about pinky pirates: They are all allergic to silver, so they have to be kept away from the adjusting screw.

In addition to bow hold, teaching students (except for bass players) to use full bows is always a challenge. Make them actually start at the frog by doing a "frog check." If they can reach out and touch a string with their right index finger, then they are really at the frog. If not, they need to move their bow. Another fun exercise to have students do is what we call "gummy bear bows." This works best for violin/viola, but cello/bass can participate for fun. Have students lick a gummy bear and stick it to the back of their right hand. Have students play a down-bow and then an up-bow on open strings. At the end of the up-bow, if they can reach the gummy bear on their hand without moving that hand, they get to eat it! This shows them that most of the time, they aren't actually getting back to the frog by the end of their up-bows.

Set-up/Fundamentals: Instrument Position and Body Alignment

In our set-up process, we have assigned numbers to each step. Before you begin the set-up itself, ask violin and viola students to trace with their right index finger the triangle from the front of their left shoulder to the back of the left shoulder to the neck. Model the tracing for them. We call this the Bermuda Triangle. This is fun because you can have a brief discussion of what allegedly happens in the real Bermuda Triangle. Next, tell them that they are going to make the Bermuda Triangle disappear by covering it with their instruments. Finally, invite them to stand and follow these steps:

1. Hold their instrument straight out in front of them, left hand on the neck, right hand on the jaw rest.
2. Lift their instruments over their heads with the scroll to the left.
3. Turn their instruments so the jaw rest is towards them.
4. Lower their instruments, landing them on their shoulders.

For cellos and basses, the steps are as follows:

1. Hold their instruments straight out in front of them with the endpin placed at the correct distance. Cellists should have their feet flat on the floor; basses should be seated on a stool with their right foot on the floor.
2. Bring their instruments toward their bodies (as opposed to leaning toward their instruments).
3. Extend their left arms to the left. (We call this the "feel for rain.")
4. Place their left hands on the fingerboard in position. If you haven't introduced positions yet, ask them to place hands on the upper bout.

This process keeps instruments and students in proper positions. You will have to help a couple of students that get twisted up like a pretzel, but for the most part, this works great no matter how large the class. After the first couple of times you model for them and walk them through the steps, they will be able to follow the numbered steps much more quickly. Eventually you can wean them off the steps altogether, but if posture becomes less than perfect, use them again.

Here are a couple of our other posture games:

- **"POP!"** "POP" stands for "Perfect Orchestra Posture." When conductors say that word, students are to stand up as quickly as possible without having to move their feet. If they are on the front half of their chair with their feet flat on the floor, they should be able to do this easily.
- **"Love your cello; don't eat your cello."** When we say this, it reminds students to have their instrument at their chests instead of their bellies.
- **"My Bonnie" Game.** This is a great game to play before students even have instruments. Teach them the song, "My Bonnie Lies Over the Ocean." Tell them to stand up on every word that begins with the letter "B." You can get faster and faster, and it becomes quite frantic and fun.

Ensemble Playing: Unity, Precision, Tempo Stability

Every ensemble is different. We have conducted groups of 140 students that played with machinelike precision, and we have struggled to help just two students play together well. The difference? Bow placement. It's just like real estate: location, location, location. It is important to start training our students early and often that bow placement matters. We try to teach students about the one-inch rule (an idea stolen about fifteen years ago after observing an all-state rehearsal). The basic premise is that everyone playing passages with a similar rhythm should be within one inch of bow placement as all the other players. Not only will it help with ensemble precision and execution; it will also force students to pay attention to each other.

Another method is to ask students to try passages in different parts of the bow and respond with input on which ways sounded the most precise and felt the most comfortable.

In addition to bow placement, teaching students to subdivide is imperative. One way to help them understand this is to have them play out the subdivisions in certain sections. For instance, if they have half notes, have them play quarters or eighths for every half note. Then you can have half the group do play the subdivided version and half play as written. Switch the groups the next time around.

You can also teach your students to move and breathe like a chamber ensemble, no matter the size of the group. Have them lean forward to feel a crescendo and back away to feel a decrescendo. Moving musically is a skill that must be taught like any other one and should be started with beginners.

Another trick to establish rhythmic stability with beginners is to "cheat." For example, in a section of sixteenth notes, have half the students play as written and ask the other half of the ensemble to play every other note— i.e., eighth notes.

Finally, pizzicato passages always prove treacherous for precision. Don't be afraid to rehearse with a metronome, and, most importantly, don't forget to have students play the passage arco as a rehearsal technique.

Expression: Phrasing, Balance, Dynamic Contrast
Balance. It might sound overly simplified, but the easiest way to teach students to learn to balance is to teach them to listen. They should be able to hear their section—not just themselves—while also listening for the melody. In order for this to work, they need to know what the melody sounds like. Ask the section with the melody to play it for the group. Then, add the other parts back in. Poll the students to see if they could hear the melody. If the non-melodic sections are still too loud, ask them to pluck their parts while the melody plays arco.

Dynamic Contrast. Achieving dynamic contrast is important, but it is important to teach students a variety of ways to do this other than just by adding or releasing weight in the bow. Assigning dynamic levels to different parts of the string (some conductors assign "lane numbers") is a quick and efficient way for students to learn about bow placement as it relates to dynamic levels. We also have luck asking students to visualize the subtle differences in dynamics by using paint swatch samples. The lighter color represents the softer dynamic level and the darker colors the louder. This activity seems to help the visual learner "see" the differences in dynamics.

I would put vibrato in this category as well, but, of course, it fits in others, too. Although vibrato is personal, the basics can be taught and worked on in a large setting. Here are some tools you can pass out to students in a group setting to help them learn vibrato:

- Felt (for "polishing" the strings)
- Film canisters filled with rice to use as shakers: Shake the canisters with different rhythms at different tempos. Also, small candy boxes (like those that come with Nerds or Tic-Tacs) can be used instead of film canisters.
- Small bouncy balls (violin/viola) and tennis balls (for cellos) to help their left hands rock and roll for vibrato motion
- Metronome for slow-motion vibrato: Set different metronome marking goals.

Some other ideas for training student vibrato include:

- Daily vibrato minute: Set a timer, then walk around the room helping individuals with vibrato.
- Proximity to a rock star: Put a student that is struggling with vibrato next to a student that has a great one, and you will be amazed at the results.

Whatever you choose to do, don't leave it up to the private teacher because most kids don't have one!

Articulation Control

One of the fundamental rules we try to teach students about any articulation is to start from the string. So often groups aren't together because they do not start with their bow on the string. Another thing we tend to nag our students about is creating a full staccato tone. Often students use a tiny amount of bow and come to a screeching halt. Alternately, try to encourage students to use a lot of bow, to move it quickly, and to make space between the notes. It creates a more resonant staccato sound and prevents the rushing issues that most assuredly will occur if students are using smaller amounts of bow.

The quickest, most effective way for our students to play spiccato is to start with eight notes on the string, then eight notes off. You can vary the number of notes if you prefer.

If you're interested in adding some technology to your class, there is a great program called Intonia that allows students to compare their dynamics, to see how even their accents are, or to compare other kinds of bow strokes.

Repertoire

Choose repertoire that will:

- reinforce the techniques and skills your group has been working on
- be enjoyable for the students (and for you)
- provide opportunities to apply concepts to future repertoire

Remember to highlight the strengths of your group. If you have a hotshot viola section, there are great pieces to feature them. With so much great literature to choose from, it can be overwhelming to decide what to play. Go to concerts and reading sessions at conferences, troll music websites during the summer to listen to pieces, and take note of pieces you hear at festivals, evaluations, competitions, or even on your local classical station.

Here's a list of ten tried-and-true pieces for a middle school orchestra:

- "Canyon Sunset," by John Caponegro
- "Spartacus," by Brian Balmages
- "Fiddling A-Round," by John Caponegro
- "Dramatic Essay," by Mark Williams
- "Night Shift," by Richard Meyer
- "Lullaby," by William Hofeldt
- "Arioso," by Michael Hopkins
- "Impravada," by David Shaffer
- "Sword Dance," arr. Bob Phillips
- "Night Rider," by Richard Meyer

Recruiting/Community Building

When our school has its official recruiting time with rising sixth graders, we make sure they hear a fun, high-quality performance from students and that they have hands-on time with instruments in an "instrument petting zoo." Your older students will enjoy helping with this event and can be your best recruiters. Our school gave a music department t-shirt to every rising sixth grader that joined one of our programs, and the students have worn them all year long. It gives them an immediate feeling of belonging at their new school.

Other methods of improving your recruiting are to make sure your performances are always of a high quality and to get your group out in your school and community. A big schoolwide project we once took on was having students sign up to play "Happy Birthday" in groups of four or five members for faculty and staff birthdays. We have been so well-received, and frequent, small performances like that allow for plenty of opportunities for any of your students to shine.

A great way we get our students out performing in the community every year is through "marching" (we use that term loosely) our eighth graders in a local parade each fall. We pass out candy and play fiddle tunes. The kids watching the parade see stringed instruments in person, and our kids feel like rock stars. It is also something our sixth and seventh graders look forward to doing before and during their time in our ensembles.

The key is to remember that students and parents talk. If they have a good experience in your program, they will be your best recruiters!

Don Brubaker

> "There are few greater privileges than touching the souls of middle school students while teaching them to make music on a string instrument."

Don Brubaker, *a native of Roanoke, Virginia, began musical studies on the violin at the age of six and on the piano and trumpet at the age of twelve. He holds a bachelor's degree in music education from West Virginia University and a master's degree in music education from the University of Illinois. In addition to his music education studies, Mr. Brubaker holds a Master of Divinity from Regent University. Mr. Brubaker has taught orchestra in the public schools of Virginia at the elementary, middle, and high school levels since 1980. In addition, he has taught band at the elementary level and has directed a private music teaching studio. He has served as a guest conductor and adjudicator throughout the state of Virginia and is a published composer of school orchestra music. In 1999, Mr. Brubaker moved to Charlottesville, Virginia to serve as orchestra director at Buford Middle School. Under Mr. Brubaker's direction, the Buford orchestra has consistently received Superior ratings and first-place awards at festivals and competitions. In addition to his work in the Charlottesville City Schools, he conducts the Evans Youth Orchestra, a junior high full orchestra associated with the Youth Orchestras of Central Virginia. In his spare time Mr. Brubaker takes trumpet lessons and plays the trumpet in the Charlottesville Municipal Band, the Charlottesville*

Brass Quintet, and the Salute to Swing jazz band. He lives in Albemarle County with his wife Gayle, a piano and voice teacher. They have three grown children and one grandchild.

Rehearsal Philosophy

I believe that playing in a school orchestra is one of the most valuable experiences for middle school students. This is where their minds, bodies, spirits, and emotions are engaged in a group activity that has no rival in their school day. Consequently, the orchestra rehearsal environment can and should be one of total student engagement. Middle school students engage and learn best in a well-defined daily rehearsal structure so that they know what to expect and what is expected of them. Once the structure is established, it can then be modified as needed in order to provide variety and freshness to the rehearsal. Thus, my goal in each rehearsal is to create a *well-structured environment* where every player is *engaged* in the process of music-making/learning and also *enjoying* that process. I tell my students on the first day of school that my two highest values as an orchestra teacher are *excellence* and *fun*! If one of these values is missing in a rehearsal, then my students are not experiencing all that I desire for them (and they're either having fun at the expense of learning or they're playing well but not enjoying it). My ultimate goal is to develop a culture of individual and group success that fosters in my students a love of good music and a love for music-making that takes them through high school and beyond.

Rehearsal Preparation

I prepare for three components in my rehearsals.

- **Warm-ups and fundamentals.** These are daily routines that review the fundamentals of rhythm and bowing patterns, finger patterns, tone and dynamics, bowing styles, vibrato, and shifting. Most of these routines are memorized by the students. This becomes very valuable in the warm-up room prior to a concert, assessment, or contest; I am able to warm up the group and remind them of the fundamentals without music stands. I use a rotational system so that the fundamentals—keystone habits of excellence—are reinforced every day. I may also use a particular warm-up or routine if it prepares for that rehearsal's primary goal.

- **Technique.** After the warm-up routines, I plan for the assessment and development of a particular aspect of playing technique (e.g., upper positions, shifting, vibrato, spiccato). I typically use a method book or technique book for this and plan to spend a few minutes assessing prior learning before progressing further with the skill. I usually plan to spend about 10–15 minutes per rehearsal on technique development unless we're approaching a performance.
- **Specific goals in one or two performance pieces.** These goals may be either sections of the piece(s) (e.g., measures 17–34) or a musical component to be applied to the entire piece (e.g., dynamics).

Before I give the students a new piece of music, I play through each part (violin I, violin II, viola, cello, and bass) and add any bowings and fingerings that are needed so that the students are playing identical bowings and fingerings within their sections. I also frequently indicate bowing styles, articulations, and bow placements (frog, middle, tip) in the parts. I make copies of these parts for the students to use at home, and I also provide the original parts (with markings) for their class folders. This takes *a lot* of prep time, but the process also prepares me to the point that I know the score by heart and have learned where any problem spots might be, thus saving me time later on. From this point, I develop strategies on how best to teach any difficult rhythms, notes, bowings, or articulations, and I look for ways to efficiently teach these spots in a piece. For example, I might play the melody with the articulations I want and then ask the students to find where the melody occurs in their parts.

Warm-Up

I am eternally grateful to Michael Allen for publishing his *Daily Warm-Ups for String Orchestra* (Hal Leonard). This set of warm-ups is four pages long and covers most of the fundamentals required for successful string playing. My intermediate orchestra (seventh grade) learns and memorizes *Daily Warm-Ups* page 1 (eighth/sixteenth/triplet rhythm patterns and the four basic finger patterns) at the beginning of the school year. After our fall concert in November, this group learns and memorizes *Daily Warm-Ups* page 2 (seven bowing styles). My advanced orchestra (seventh and eighth grade) plays either page 1 or page 2 each day. Once they are comfortable with shifting, they learn *Daily Warm-Ups* page 3, which has excellent exercises for double stops, tone development, string crossings, and shifting. Once this group knows all three pages, then I just rotate through the pages, playing one page per rehearsal. (I reserve *Daily Warm-Ups* page 4 for when the students reach high school.) This resource gives the middle school orchestra teacher the ability to quickly reinforce fundamental concepts of playing each day at the beginning of rehearsal. With some creativity, the *Daily Warm-Ups* can be varied and, as stated earlier, becomes invaluable right before a performance.

After the *Daily Warm-Ups*, I teach/reinforce rhythm reading with either a rhythm book, a sight-reading book, or PowerPoint slides. If there is time, this may be followed with brief shifting or vibrato preparatory exercises. At the conclusion of the warm-up part of the rehearsal, I lead the students through a few seconds of stretches to prepare their muscles for the rest of the rehearsal.

Intonation and Fluency: Developing the Left Hand
Intonation is one of the most challenging aspects of string-playing/teaching and requires constant vigilance by the teacher/conductor. In order to develop good intonation in my students, I introduce the four basic finger patterns and reinforce them daily. (My students usually come to me knowing one or two of the finger patterns.) I name the finger patterns based on the nomenclature in Gazda and Stoutamire's *Spotlight on Strings* (Kjos) method book:

- **The Major Finger Pattern:** the first five notes of the major scale starting on an open string
  Example: D E F♯ ^ G A
  Basses shift to third position on the fourth note: 0 1 4 -1 4
- **The Minor Finger Pattern:** the first five notes of the minor scale starting on an open string
  Example: D E ^ F G A
  Basses shift to third position on the fourth note: 0 1 2 -1 4
- **The Forward Extension Finger Pattern:** the major finger pattern with fourth note sharped
  Example: D E F♯ G♯ ^ A
  Violins and violas extend 3rd finger toward 4th finger
  Cellos play F♯ with extended 2nd finger, G♯ with 4th finger
  Basses shift to third position on the fourth note: 0 1 4 -2 4

- **The Back Extension Finger Pattern:** the minor FP with first
  finger back a half-step
  Example: D ^ E♭ F G A
  *Basses play E♭ F G in half position, then shift to third position
  for G A*

Once a new finger pattern is learned, I have the students sing the note names on each string while playing pizzicato. This—plus using echo playing with each finger pattern—helps to develop the students' audiation and pitch-matching skills. I also teach the students to listen for the sympathetic vibration (or "ring") that is produced when a fingered note has a corresponding open string. This ring is especially obvious at the octave (e.g., D on the A string causes a dramatic ringing vibration of the D string). I allow the students to experiment with finding the ringing tones on their instruments, and I encourage them to listen as they move their fingers sharper or flatter as the ring appears and disappears.

In order to develop harmonic intonation, the group plays the finger patterns and scales in rounds so that they can learn to place their notes harmonically as well as melodically. When rehearsing a piece, I will stop and hold a note or chord in order to lock in the intonation on that note or chord. I often play the note on the violin so that the pitch can be accurately heard and matched. Sometimes it is necessary to stop and hold several notes in a difficult phrase or sequence in order to ensure that everyone is matching pitch. This is especially needed with tricky shifts!

I use *Essential Technique for Strings* (Hal Leonard) to teach shifting and upper positions. I have recorded and uploaded each position/shifting exercise onto the orchestra's website so that the students can practice with the recording at home and match pitch. For both shifting and vibrato, I prefer to introduce these concepts with the violin and viola students in guitar position, which allows them to see their left hands better and makes them less likely to shift or vibrate with tension.

In order to develop fluency and accuracy in fast passages I often use the following routine. If the notes are grouped in fours, each group of four notes is played like this:

- *Fast—slow—slow—slow* for the entire passage; then
- *Fast—fast—slow—slow*; then
- *Fast—fast—fast—slow*; and finally
- *Fast—fast—fast—fast.*

The same idea is applied if the notes are grouped in sixes (as in 6/8). If needed, the routine can be done again with longer groupings of notes. If the passage contains slurs, I find it helpful to develop left-hand rhythmic accuracy with separate bows before adding the slurs.

Tone: Developing the Right Hand and Bow Control
My students come to me with their bow holds already set but usually needing refinement. I encourage them to keep their right thumbs and fingers flexible by doing thumb taps and "pinkie push-ups." These little 10-second actions can be sprinkled throughout the rehearsal. I take the opportunity at the beginning of each rehearsal to check the students' bowing (Is it straight with full bows?) while I check their tuning (four quarter-note full bows on each open string). I also use this time to teach/reinforce bow placement, bow speed, and arm weight for the various dynamic levels. I use three lanes: near the fingerboard for *pp* and *p*, in the middle for *mp* and *mf*, near the bridge for *f* and *ff*. In order to help the students conceptualize playing into the string with a resonant tone, I ask them to make their bows "sticky" and wiggle the string with the bow without producing a sound. Once they release the string to produce the tone, it is usually firm and resonant instead of wimpy or glassy. I can then say "Use sticky bows" when rehearsing, and they immediately know what to do. So that the students can learn how to really play *f* and *ff*, I may have them crunch the string at the beginning of a note and then back off just a little to maintain the volume but to lose the crunching sound. Combined with a fast bow speed at the beginning of the note, this procedure can help produce nice accents and **martelé** bowing.

There are seven bowing styles found on the second page of Allen's *Daily Warm-Ups*. These seven styles are spiccato, slurred staccato, retake, grand **martelé**, hooked, **louré**, and tremolo. Once the students know these bowing styles (and play them at least every other day), it is easy to incorporate them in the music being rehearsed. The time spent on the bowing styles unit and the warm-up routine pays great dividends when the music requires something more than **detaché**, slurs, or staccato.

Once bow control is set and the bowing styles are learned, I teach the students to tilt the bow in order to refine the bow stroke and produce a more even sound from frog to tip. The players tilt the bow stick away from the bridge at the frog—playing on the side of the hair—and gradually flatten the bow hair toward the middle of the bow.

Set-Up/Fundamentals: Instrument Position and Body Alignment
Since my students come to me having already played for a year or two, I don't have the privilege of establishing their set-up and the fundamentals of hand positions. Most of what I do is either remediation or reinforcement of prior learning. I encourage violinists and violists to place the instrument high enough on the shoulder so that they can easily point their left elbows to their left knees. I encourage cellists and bassists to balance the instrument so that it comes to them and not vice versa. All of this requires good posture, which I check at the beginning of each rehearsal (back straight, feet flat on the floor). I like to use short and quick verbal cues throughout rehearsals to remind the students of proper hand positions and posture— "back straight," "feet flat," "thumb up" (for violin/viola left hand position), "elbow up" (for cello/bass left hand position).

Ensemble Playing: Unity, Precision, Tempo Stability
As with most things, ensemble technique grows out of the daily fundamentals. The rhythm patterns on page 1 of *Daily Warm-Ups*, often accompanied by an amplified metronome, help establish rhythmic precision and unity throughout the group early in the school year. I stress that everyone must play with the same tempo and articulation in the warm-ups (after I demonstrate on the violin what I want them to do), and then I expect that same level of conformity in all of the music we rehearse. I find that there is no substitute for modeling the precision I desire, so I will often play with the students when we're learning a new piece so that they can hear and watch me and then match my style and articulation (as well as intonation).

There are several techniques that I often employ during rehearsals to bring clarity to "muddy" or difficult passages:

- **Pizzicato.** When students play any rhythm pizzicato, they are forced to commit to a specific time to play each note. In other words, they can't fake the rhythm as easily as they can when playing arco. It also gives me the opportunity to hear better what the problem might be if I don't already know. I also find that the violin/viola students are more able to count out loud while playing pizzicato in guitar position than when playing arco. Pizzicato with counting often solves the problem. It allows each player to focus on the notes and rhythm without dealing with bowing.

- **Air bowing.** Once the rhythm and notes are secure with pizzicato, air bowing helps isolate any bowing issues that might be affecting precision. Bow direction, length of bow, and bow lifts can be addressed without the distraction of the left hand. The air bowing I use is vertical—straight up and down—rather than horizontal.

- **Subdivision.** I find that many rhythmic inaccuracies with middle school orchestras occur during long notes and rests. It is typical for young players to shave time off of anything longer than a quarter note or to come in early after a rest. Subdividing helps by filling in the gaps created by longer notes and rests. But it must be a physical action—counting out loud and/or playing the subdivision (e.g., playing half notes as four eighth notes). Hopefully, this will lead the players to feel the subdivision inside their heads when playing the notes as written. Subdividing with a metronome is also invaluable for keeping the tempo from rushing when the group is playing staccato or pizzicato. They must get used to hearing and feeling the space between the short notes.

- **Bow stops.** Tied eighth notes or sixteenth notes and dotted quarter notes often present precision problems for young players. Depending on the tempo and style of the piece, this can be solved by asking the players to stop the bow on the tied note or the dot (actually playing a rest instead of the tied note or dot). Musically, this makes sense, since the place of the stopped bow is probably where a wind player or singer would take a breath. In many cases, the notes that follow the tie actually begin a new phrase in the music.

Expression: Phrasing, Balance, Dynamic Contrast

Musical phrasing is what keeps music from sounding mechanical, and dynamics are the building blocks of phrasing. I teach my students how to play various dynamic levels (*pp* to *ff*) by showing them how to apply the variables of bow speed, bow length, bow placement, and arm weight in order to produce the desired dynamic. Once they are comfortable performing each dynamic level on open strings (while I point to a dynamic marking on the board), I then incorporate dynamics into their *Daily Warm-Ups* and method book material. After this is solid, I add crescendo and decrescendo to the open string warm-ups, *Daily Warm-Ups*, and method book songs.

Phrasing, like everything else, needs to be taught to young players until it becomes intuitive. One advantage that young wind players have over young string players is that they need to take a breath, and the breathing points are usually determined by the phrase (just like they are when one is speaking). However, string players have to be taught how and where to "breathe" with the bow. I do this by having my students sing/hum the phrase and breathe at the end of phrases. (For some students, it helps to pretend they're playing a wind instrument such as a recorder.) When using the bow, the end of the phrase can be executed with a bow lift or slight stop of the bow (usually after a decrescendo). Once the bow breaths are set, then the shape of the phrase is determined by the rise and fall of the melodic line—a little crescendo on the way up the line and a little decrescendo on the way down. All of this is modeled for the students in a call-and-response fashion until everyone is able to produce a melodic phrase (usually a bit exaggerated).

Most concert pieces I program contain melodic material written for each section of the orchestra. Once the students determine where in the piece they have the melody, I play the phrases for them the way they should sound. Then, I instruct them to make an arc through the air with their hands for each phrase that I am playing. Next, they play the melodic line with me until they are comfortable with the phrasing and the style. By working on the melody together, we waste less rehearsal and individual practice, and students develop a better sense of when they have the melody and who has it when they do not. At this point, we can work on the accompanying material in the piece with the understanding that it should be played underneath the melody for the sake of balance. If the students have difficulty remembering to play louder for the melody and softer for the accompaniment, I have them either write in the dynamics needed at each spot or indicate in their parts where they have the melody.

As I mentioned above, I find it helpful to have the students slightly stop the bow on tied and dotted notes, especially if the tie or dot comes at the end of a phrase. For other ideas on phrasing and musical expression I highly recommend Kenneth Laudermilch's *An Understandable Approach to Musical Expression* (2000, Meredith Music Publications). This short text is written for all instrumentalists and specifies the artistic concepts that competent musicians should know in order to become expressive players.

Articulation Control
Once my students learn the seven bowing styles of *Daily Warm-Ups* page 2, we review them at least every other day. This consistent practice gives my students increased comfort and confidence with each bowing style. After several weeks, they are ready to apply these skills to any music they encounter at their level. They also know what I'm talking about when I ask them to use a particular bowing style (e.g., martelé or louré). One word regarding spiccato: I like to make sure that the students keep the bow close to the string and don't bounce too high.

Repertoire
When selecting repertoire for my middle school orchestras, I look for three things in each piece: playability, musicality, and educational value. The key, rhythms, meter, tempo, and technique must be within the comfort range of most of the players while still giving them the opportunity to grow. If the piece is too difficult, they will not perform it well, and it will be a negative experience for them. If it is too easy, they will not grow from it and will quickly become bored. Musically, the piece must have interesting melodic, rhythmic, and harmonic elements for each section of the orchestra (not just first violins) while staying within the technical capabilities of the group. At this level I especially like to include various folk styles—Celtic, Spanish, bluegrass, jazz, etc., as well as more common orchestral composers like Vivaldi. I also want the piece to introduce or reinforce the educational goals of my curriculum—a recently learned key, rhythm pattern, or technique. (For example, Doug Spata's *Agincourt* is a wonderful way to introduce middle school players to 7/8!) The bottom line for me is that I must really like the piece. It should be one that I will enjoy teaching and that my students will enjoy learning.

I believe that it is also important to keep in mind the overall program for a concert when selecting repertoire. I like for a program to include various styles, modes, keys, and tempi. To help me plan each concert, I developed a concert template that suggests where to place the pieces in the program. Careful consideration should especially be given to the opening and closing selections of a concert. I prefer for the first piece to serve as a warm-up with an easy key, a moderate-to-fast tempo, and some unison rhythms. This builds the confidence of each student and prepares them for the rest of the concert. The concert closer is usually a bold and exciting piece that the students love to play and brings the audience to their feet.

An Annotated List of Recommended Middle School String Orchestra Pieces
- "Saliendo," by S. Day (grade 2–3; beautiful, relaxed piece in a Spanish style)
- "Goin' to Boston," by C.L. Gruselle (grade 2; a fun fiddle tune that makes an excellent warm-up piece)
- "Russian Sailor's Dance," by R. Gliere/DelBorgo (grade 3; nice variations on this classic)
- "El Toro," by D. Brubaker (often listed as grade 2, but I think it's a 3 if played up to tempo; includes solo violin/cello)
- "For the Star of County Down," arr. D.B. Monday (beautiful medley of Irish tunes; easy grade 4)
- "Variations on a Sailing Song," arr. C. Strommen (wonderful grade 3; great warm-up piece)
- "Conquistador," by D.B. Monday (grade 3, Spanish flavor)
- "M to the Third Power," by C. Nunez (grade 3–4; uses changing meter, very cool)
- "Fantasy on a Japanese Folk Song," by B. Balmages (lovely grade 3; this one looks easy but requires sensitivity/control)
- "Ellis Island," by A.L. Silva (grade 4; contemporary sounding piece with a Celtic flair)
- "Baroque Encounter," by R. Stephan (grade 3; effectively combines Baroque and blues elements)
- "Nobody Knows the Trouble I've Seen," arr. C.L. Gruselle. (grade 3–4; excellent treatment of the spiritual with nice solos)
- Concerto Grosso Opus 6, No. 2, mvt. IV, by Handel/Dackow (nice grade 4 of this style)

- "Allegro in D," by Vivaldi/Frackenpohl (grade 4 arrangement of Vivaldi's concerto for two trumpets; fun to play)
- "Dance of the Tumblers," by Rimsky-Korsakov/Dackow (grade 3–4; off-beats toward the end are challenging; good opener)
- "Pyramids," by R. Frost (wonderful grade 4 with lots of rhythmic interest)
- "Vortex," by R. Longfield (grade 4; nice overture feel (ABA) in a driving minor key)
- "Momentum," by R. Longfield (grade 4; similar to "Vortex")
- "Agincourt," by D. Spata (grade 3 in 7/8! very cool; has wonderful viola part)
- "Prelude" from the *Holberg Suite*, by Grieg/B. McBrien (good grade 4 arrangement of this)
- Selections from *West Side Story,* L. Bernstein/J. Moss (grade 3–4; Moss has several arrangements of WSS—all outstanding)
- "Somewhere" from *West Side Story*, Bernstein/Moss (beautiful lengthened arrangement from the above)
- "American Reel," by K. Mosier (really nice grade 4 Celtic fiddle piece with violin solo/duet and cool countermelody in cello/bass)
- "Solace," by S. Joplin/R. Longfield (excellent grade 3–4 adaptation of this ragtime standard)
- "Allegro for Strings" (from Sonata Op. 1, No. 3), by Handel/Frackenpohl (a good grade 4 standard)
- "Eine Kleine Nachtmusik," by Mozart/Isaac (a grade 4 standard work horse; an abridgement of the original)
- "Rocken," by S.J. Atwell (grade 4; well-written piece with rock/blues elements throughout; cool cello/bass parts)
- "The Sprint," by A.L. Silva (an up-tempo grade 4 where every section gets lots of action)
- "Ruminations," by S. O'Loughlin (a grade 3 with gorgeous harmonies; looks easy but requires stellar intonation/tone)
- "Palladio," by K. Jenkins/R. Longfield (a nice grade 3–4 arrangement if the group isn't quite ready for the original)
- "Hungarian Dance No. 5," by Brahms/Isaac (a grade 4 standard classic)
- "Three Slavonic Dances," by Dvořák/Isaac (another grade 4 standard classic)

- "When Johnny Comes Marching Home," arr. R. Stephan (an old classic grade 3; well-written; requires mutes)
- "Fantasia on a Theme from Thailand," by R. Meyer (wonderful grade 3–4; lots of interesting musical elements)

Recruiting/Community Building

The personal connection I develop with students helps many of them to comfortably make the transition to the next orchestra.

Because I don't teach beginners in my school district, I don't have primary recruiting responsibilities. (That falls to the teacher in the upper-elementary school that feeds my middle school.) However, I do see it as my responsibility to help the students already in the orchestra program to move up to the next level in the program, especially from one school to the next. To this end, I teach a two-week summer orchestra program that is open to all orchestra students in rising grades 5–7. This is an opportunity for me to work with students who will one day be in my program. The personal connection I develop with them helps many of them to comfortably make the transition to seventh-grade orchestra.

On the other end, I desire to see all of my eighth-grade students transition to the high school orchestra program. To accomplish this, I invite the high school orchestra director and the top orchestra at the high school to join my orchestra in our annual fall concert. At this concert, my students perform their program and then get to listen to the high school orchestra perform one piece. Then, the grand finale of the concert is a combined piece where both my advanced orchestra and the high school advanced orchestra are conducted by the high school director in a side-by-side situation. This experience gives my students a good feel for the high school program so that they desire to continue playing in orchestra in high school.

The most important event of my school year is the orchestra's annual spring trip. This trip involves a competition in the morning followed by an afternoon in an amusement park. The students look forward to this day (usually a school day) and are motivated to meet the requirements to participate. These requirements include attending all after-school rehearsals and successfully playing all concert music. I have found the spring trip to be especially beneficial for students who are borderline in the orchestra program (usually due to inadequate effort). Once they truly apply them-selves (because they want to go on the trip!), these students learn the joy of excellence and are motivated to continue playing. And for all of my students, the camaraderie developed during the preparation for and the participation in the trip is invaluable.

Seth Gamba

"Never stop counting!"

Seth Gamba teaches orchestra at Elkins Pointe Middle School in the Atlanta area. He has a degree in double bass performance and civics from Indiana University and a Master of Music Education from the University of Georgia. He has many works published for string orchestra, as well a collection of supplemental rhythm exercises called Rhythmic Projections and two collections of ensemble music for student-level bass players. He has given presentations at Midwest, ASTA, NAfME, TMEA, OMEA, and GMEA, as well as for several local school districts.

Rehearsal Philosophy

The expectations and goals of a heterogeneous orchestra class are different from those of a professional rehearsal. There's a saying that's been around for a long time: Rehearsal is where you go to learn everyone else's part, not your own. While this may be true of a professional ensemble and mostly true of a collegiate ensemble, it is not really true in K–12 orchestra rooms. This is not to say that I never trot out that line from time to time to make a point about practicing. It's more that I know that my role in the classroom is mostly as a teacher and only very little as a conductor.

I never showed up for a private lesson and had my teacher explain to me that he wasn't there to teach me how to play my parts. Of course, there was the expectation that I would put in my time practicing my instrument,

48

but my private lesson teachers spent a lot of time showing me how to do things. In the later stages of learning a piece, we would, of course, get to the finer points of musical expression. After the jury or recital was over, though, we would start the process over with new material. I think of my orchestra classes more as private lessons with a lot of students at once than I think of them as professional-style rehearsals.

My students are in orchestra to learn how to play instruments. I am there to teach them how to play instruments. To learn how to play an instrument, a student must spend a lot of time playing the instrument. This is my prime directive in running an orchestra class: Keep everyone playing their instrument for as much of the time as possible. Strive for the minimum possible amount of downtime in a class. My second goal is to make sure that everyone is together all of the time. I emphasize to my students that great music happens when people play it together and that everyone's sound matters. I refuse to start the music unless everyone is ready.

The main focus of most classes is on skill development. The ultimate goal is to play great music, but that can only happen if students are making progress developing their skills on their instruments. Sometimes we are learning a brand new skill. More often, we are consolidating, deepening, and applying skills that we already have at some level. I try to go into each class with a short list of the skills that will be the focus of the lesson.

I try to limit instructions to one or two steps, and then start playing. This helps keep everyone engaged and feeling like they're moving forward. It also really helps with the discipline problems that can crop up when you have a large group of kids together. One of the most common problems I see when I observe new teachers in any subject is that they give too many instructions at once before the students begin. When given too many steps or instructions to remember, students feel lost, get distracted, stop paying attention, start talking to their neighbors, and all manner of other things that ultimately mean you will have to go over all of it again anyway.

Rehearsal Preparation
Rehearsal preparation begins with careful selection of repertoire. I think of each concert cycle as a unit in the same way that a science, math, ELA, or

social studies teacher might. The repertoire selected will determine the focus of the unit. It is critical to select repertoire that will give you the opportunities to focus on the skills that your students need to be working on.

I generally structure my lessons into three parts: 1) warm-ups, 2) something new, and 3) something long-term. For warm-ups, I consider what skills we need to focus on so that our concert music will turn out great. I review and work on deepening these skills in the context of the warm-up. I always follow this with something new. I use what I call "short-term pieces" for this spot in the lesson. These are short pieces taken from a variety of method books and short piece collections. They are not intended for performance, and they are selected so that students can master them in a week or less. They are also selected to apply the skills needed in the concert repertoire in a variety of contexts. Since each book generally only has a few selections that focus on a particular skill, I keep class sets of several books to pass out and take up as needed for short-term pieces.

I always end the lesson with work on concert repertoire. Early in the concert cycle, I tend to spend the bulk of each lesson on the warm-up and short-term pieces while we learn and develop the skills that are needed for the concert repertoire. As the concert gets closer, that balance shifts so that the bulk of the rehearsal time is spent on the concert repertoire.

To meet my prime directive of keeping everyone playing their instruments, I create "theme sheets" for each piece of concert repertoire. The theme sheet consists of all of the melodies, main harmonies, and anything else that I anticipate causing difficulty for my students. All of those parts are put into all clefs and transposed appropriately for each instrument. As we rehearse the repertoire, single sections almost never play alone. When we hit a hard spot, we switch over to the theme sheet and everyone learns the parts in unison. The result of this has been more even skill development across different instruments in my groups, fewer discipline problems, and better balance as students are better at listening to each other's parts when they play.

Warm-Up
Sometimes we feel pressed for time, but please take my advice and *never skip scales*! All music is made of scales and arpeggios. When students

have a solid command of their scale and arpeggio patterns and can recognize them when they show up in their repertoire, they learn faster and play more in tune.

Scale practice also provides the perfect time to teach and refine new techniques as well as to reteach skills that some students never quite owned. If students are playing something they know how to do really well, it frees their mental resources to focus on the new skills in isolation, rather than having to do that along with learning a whole new piece of music. It is important, though, to mix up what you do with the scales. Sometimes the focus is on perfect tuning; at other times, the focus can be on a new bow stroke, full tone, dynamic changes, tempo changes, rhythms, bowing patterns, or almost anything you can think of.

I teach students all seven modes of the D scale. In this way, I can use the D scale to teach all of the basic finger patterns to everyone at the same time without having to worry about the range issues that come with moving to different major keys. Once students can play all seven modes at will, it is very easy to expand that into the seven major scales between E♭ and A. It also lays the groundwork for quick and easy understanding of the concept of parallel and relative keys.

Intonation and Fluency: Developing the Left Hand
Many tuning problems begin with technical problems. If the instrument is not being held correctly or if the left hand is not shaped correctly, anything else you do to get students to play in tune will be a waste of time. Students must sit tall, have straight wrists, tall fingers, and good thumb placement first and foremost. I am also a strong advocate of finger tapes for beginners. This gives the beginning student the ability to set their hand frame on their own without the teacher having to be there to constantly correct it. In my large, heterogeneous classes of beginners, I can't possibly give enough individual attention to get everyone's hands set without the help of finger tapes.

Once instrument position is set, the next step for solid tuning is singing. Singing is the foundation for audiation, and audiation is the foundation for good intonation. Many people have asked me over the years about how to get students to sing. The simple answer is that if you want your students to sing, *you* have to sing! Any time you say the note names of a section, sing them. Any time you have students count the rhythm of a section, sing the counting syllables on the notes.

Another tool is to emphasize to students that constantly adjusting tuning is a critical part of playing a stringed instrument. Without the aid of frets, the best we can hope for is that our good hand position will get us really close to the note that we hope to play. After that, we have to adjust. Great players don't nail every note. They just fix the notes they miss so fast that most people don't notice it. I emphasize for my students that there is a question they must ask and an answer they must have for every note they play. The question is "Am I in tune?" The answer is "Probably not, *so fix it!*" I tell them that a note that starts out of tune but gets fixed quickly is a note that was never out of tune. Praise your students lavishly when you hear them quickly fix a note that was out of tune. Your group will only really play in tune once everyone finally decides that they are probably out of tune. This mindset makes students more careful about thinking ahead to the next note, setting their hand position to be ready for it, and then making the small adjustments that are always necessary.

Tone: Developing the Right Hand and Bow Control
There are three things that affect basic tone quality on a stringed instrument: 1) bow placement (or contact point), 2) bow speed, and 3) bow weight. These three things and the ways that they interact are really the whole story. It is worth noting that some people will add bow tilt as a fourth category, but I think of tilt more as a technique used to control and vary the other factors. The way these three factors interact and are manipulated determine if your tone is focused and solid, light and wispy, thin and scratchy, or any other adjectives you'd like to apply. For a great discussion of the scientific basis of these factors, I highly recommend James Kjelland's book *Orchestral Bowing: Style and Function.*

To understand how the three factors interact, I think of the bow and string combination as a gear system. If you pluck a string and then look at the way it vibrates—starting from the bridge and going to the edge of the fingerboard—it makes the shape of a cone with the sharp point at the bridge. Now, imagine that cone as a series of different sized gears with the smallest by the bridge and the largest by the fingerboard. The "gears" are all making the same number of revolutions per second (the frequency of the pitch being played), but the string is actually moving faster at the fingerboard than it is at the bridge. This is because the cone is wider at the fingerboard and the string has more distance to cover to make the same number of revolutions per second as at the bridge where the cone is narrower.

Next, consider that the width of string vibration is what causes volume. That is, the louder you play, the wider the vibration of the string. Here is where the bow comes into play. A string will have the best basic tone when the speed of the bow matches the speed of the string. That means that to play at a certain volume, you will have to use different bow speeds depending on your bow placement. For instance, to play *mf* over the fingerboard will require a very fast bow speed. In the center lane, it will be a medium bow speed, and at the bridge, it will be a slow bow speed. If you don't match the bow speed with vibration width of the string at a certain contact point, you will get squeaks, scratches, and all manner of other tone problems. This is why a straight bow stroke is so important. When the bow is crooked, the student has a single bow speed, but the contact point is constantly changing. The changing bow placement introduces all kinds of irregularities into the vibration of the string, which leads to poor tone.

Once you understand the relationship between bow placement and bow speed and matching those to the vibration of the string, the next important thing is to know when to vary those and why. To understand this, you have to know about Helmholtz vibrations. (Look this up on YouTube!) A bowed string does not vibrate in the shape of a smooth parabola. Instead, the action of the bow grabbing and releasing the string makes a small corner that travels up and down the string. The sharpness of the corner is determined by how close to the bridge you are bowing. The sharpness of the corner also determines the mix of upper harmonic partials present in the sound. This translates roughly into tone quality that sounds more intense when bow placement is near the bridge. So if you take the *mf* from earlier and listen to its character with fast bows at the fingerboard, slow bows at the bridge, or medium bows in between, even though it's all *mf,* each one of those bowing approaches produces a different character that can be used for artistic or expressive purposes.

You may notice that I've talked mostly about placement and speed. I think of weight as the most dependent of the three factors. What you are doing with placement and speed generally determines how much weight you need. Weight becomes more of an independent factor when you begin addressing different types of articulation. Then the questions become: How much bow weight do you need to start the note? Should the bow weight be released, maintained, or increased after starting the note? If the weight is being released, how quickly should it be released? In answering these questions and controlling speed and placement, you can find virtually every sound that a bowed string instrument can produce.

Having a good bow hold and control of the bow arm is critical to controlling the three factors of placement, speed, and weight. It is important to remember what the goal is, though. I spend a lot of time helping my students get their bow holds right, but I am careful to remind them about why it really matters. When the bow hold is stiff and squeezy and the arm joints don't move fluidly, you lose control of placement, speed, and weight.

Set-Up/Fundamentals: Instrument Position and Body Alignment

Execution of all skills boils down to set-up. I was at a Q&A with violinist Leila Josefowicz following one of the most musically engaging performances I've ever heard. Someone asked her a question about practicing technique versus practicing musicality, and her answer made so much sense I was blown away by it. She said that musicality and technique are inseparable. To express a musical idea, you have to be able to manipulate your instrument physically to make it come out. In that sense, musicality *is* technique.

When I was an undergraduate, I studied bass with Larry Hurst at Indiana University. He is one of the great bass teachers of our time, with students in major symphony orchestras around the world. One of the things that made lessons with him so powerful was his ability to always bring things back to basics. No matter how advanced the concept was that we were working on, he was always able to explain how to make it happen physically on the instrument. For me, it took the answer from Leila Josefowicz to unlock in hindsight what made Larry Hurst such a great teacher.

Good set-up requires constant reminders. It is common to fall into the trap of thinking that once you've gone over something once, it will stick. From tuning to tone, most common problems begin with set-up problems, and a host of common set-up problems continually creep back into students' approaches to their instruments. It is a common problem among music teachers to focus on a note that is out of tune and not on why the note is out of tune, or to focus on a passage that needs a crescendo instead of on how to create a crescendo. All musical expression, at some level, boils down to set-up. Poor set-up will lead to frustration over time. As students mature musically, if they have poor set-up, they will hit a wall where their technique will not allow them to keep up with their vision.

Ensemble Playing: Unity, Precision, Tempo Stability
Great music happens when people play together. Jere Flint, Atlanta Symphony cellist and Atlanta Symphony Youth Orchestra director, drove home for me the importance of rhythmic precision and the fine art of fak-ing it. What he helped me realize is that if you miss a note, you sound bad for a moment, but that moment passes quickly, and then you can get back on the right note. Many times, depending on context, no one will notice the missed note. If you miss a rhythm, though, you are now in the wrong place, and *every* note you play is wrong.

For students, it is essential that rhythmic concepts are approached sepa-rately and systematically. It happens far too often that rhythm and count-ing systems are learned in the context of specific pieces and students never really understand them. Instead, they memorize new rhythms without learning how to transfer counting skills to new situations.

It is also important to understand how rhythmic precision affects tun-ing. When notes don't change precisely together, it is very difficult for an ensemble to play in tune. Imagine a measure of four quarter notes going up a scale. If some people change a little too soon and some change a little too late, then the beginnings and endings of each note are actually the interval of a second rather than a unison. This sound is incredibly hard to tune, and only a fraction of each beat of the measure can actually have clear pitch even if everyone is playing the note in tune—which is unlikely if each note starts out as some kind of second.

Once everyone is counting together, listening is key. Students must know their parts well enough that they can listen to everyone else's. In the great funk/jazz bassist Victor Wooten's book *The Music Lesson*, he writes about learning how to listen, and I got the following exercise from it: Instruct each student to pick someone across the room from themselves. Next, tell them that on this play-through, they have to listen specifically to that person as they all play together. Of course, that's not really possible, but you will be surprised at how much more everyone reacts to one another once they open their ears to everyone else around them.

Another thing that I explain to my students is that in professional ensembles, there is no expectation of steady tempo. Tempo is an element that is manipulated like any other. How, then, do you trust it will be manipulated together with 80 other people? First, you trust that everyone has great, steady time to begin with. Second, you trust that everyone is listening to one another. Finally, you trust that everyone will look up when they need to. Ideally, students will then ask, "When do we need to look up?" There are the obvious answers to this—starting points, stopping points, transition points, or known changes. The deeper answer, though, is that professionals will look up whenever they hear that the group is not together somehow, even if it's only a tiny bit. Intense listening keeps the little things that are always happening from turning into the big things that can crash a performance.

Expression: Phrasing, Balance, Dynamic Contrast
Expression is built on good set-up and solid command of fundamentals. If you have these under control, you can make musical decisions and then execute them. Once the decisions are made, active listening becomes the key. Yoel Levi, former conductor of the Atlanta Symphony, taught me a huge lesson when he conducted a piece for a concert while I was a member of the ASYO: Every note has a musical purpose. It is either going somewhere or coming back from somewhere. Never let music be static. When students know their parts, listen to each other, and are brought together in a shared vision of what the music should express, I find that the expressive aspects of a performance come together quickly.

Articulation Control

Articulation is another area that I find will generally take care of itself if you've done the groundwork correctly. That groundwork is, of course, good bow hold, understanding of how the three tone fundamentals (placement, speed, weight) interact, and strong listening skills. Teaching the basic bow strokes certainly requires some direct instruction, but if a student knows what sound they want, they will be able to get it as long as they have good enough technique to allow it. Try this: When students don't match style, don't tell them what to do. Instead, tell them to listen to each other and come to agreement. They will virtually always arrive at a matched and appropriate articulation for a section.

Repertoire

Repertoire selection is critical to ensuring the progress and interest of your students. It is also important that your repertoire fits your curriculum. If the repertoire you select doesn't support the skills that your students need to develop, includes skills only for some and not for others, or skips ahead to skills your students aren't ready for yet, you will have trouble. When I am planning a concert program, I consider five basic questions:

- Is it good music? (important to consider this from a student's perspective as well)
- Do violas and basses have interesting parts?
- What skills does it incorporate, and can my students do them?
- Will my students be able to sound good on it?
- What new things will I have to teach for it, and are my students ready to learn those skills?

If the answers don't match my expectations for an ensemble, I do not use the piece.

I was fortunate to be able to attend a workshop with Eliot Del Borgo before he passed. He made one point very strongly, and it really stuck with me. He said, "If you want your students to sound better, play easier music!" Many of us fall into the trap of over-programming for our groups. You will get better results, better attitudes, and better retention when your students are making great music. Keeping them in the sweet spot where the music is difficult enough to challenge them but easy enough that they can rise to the challenge is probably the most important thing to consider when picking repertoire.

There is always new music coming out, and, as someone who is actively writing new music and looking for music for my students to play, I've found that the quality of music for student orchestras has only been going up. I know that it can be time-consuming, but our repertoire is a large part of our curriculum. Finding the right music that will fit the needs of our ensembles is a task that never ends. Generally, *I try not to get trapped in the cycle of re*lying on the same old standards, and I am opposed to top-10 type lists. My advice is to instead listen to the publisher CDs that come out each year, never miss the opportunity to go to a music reading session, listen to other groups at performance evaluations, and take notes on what you hear. As you do those things, ask the five questions and remain open to all the possibilities.

Recruiting/Community Building

I frequently hear the trope from colleagues about how nice it must be that all of my students are in my class because they want to be there. I have to explain that this cuts both ways. I have to keep them wanting to be there. If I don't, they will leave. It is part of being a great teacher of any subject. You have to make your students excited about learning. Whether the students elected to join a class or not, a great teacher will make them want to be there.

The first step, though, is making them want to be there to start with. Be a presence at your feeder schools. Keep good relationships with the music teachers there, whether they are teaching orchestra and sending kids directly to you or teaching general music and trying to get kids excited about learning instruments as they get older. Take some student groups over to do some performances if you can. The less of a mystery you and your program are, the better you'll do getting people in the door. I am not a natural salesman, and selling my program to beginners is one of the least favorite parts of my job. Building a program requires selling the program, though. Not many people will buy a product that they haven't seen.

Once students are in your program, be reasonable. A "my way or the high-way" attitude can push people away and build resentment. Everyone has a lot going on, and some students will be more committed to the program than others. Try to find ways to give everyone a little of what they need. For some, that will just be a seat in your class. For others, that will be an advanced ensemble with extra challenging music that might have to meet before or after school. When someone comes to you with a concern, take an honest look. If they have a point, be willing to admit it and look for ways to make changes that will benefit everyone.

Sandy B. Goldie

"Play with passion, precision, and unity. Make music, not notes."

Sandy Goldie *is passionate about thriving public school orchestra programs, having worked as a public school orchestra teacher for fourteen years and with young string groups in one capacity or another for almost thirty years. She is an active guest conductor and orchestra clinician and works with honors orchestra groups and all-state orchestras across the United States, currently conducting the Richmond Symphony Concert Youth Orchestra in Richmond, VA. She has presented nationally and internationally at conferences such as ASTA, the Midwest Clinic, TMEA, ISAME, NAfME, and numerous state conferences. Dr. Goldie has served as state president of ASTA in both Virginia and South Carolina. Her book* String Instruments: Purchasing, Maintenance, Troubleshooting and More *serves as a handy classroom guide for many orchestra teachers and is used as a text in undergraduate string education courses. As a violist, she has performed professionally in symphonies in South Carolina, North Carolina, and Georgia. She is currently the string music education specialist and assistant professor of music education at Virginia Commonwealth University*

Rehearsal Philosophy

To me, music teaching is a calling—not just a job—because it has the power to transform people's lives. I seek to create meaningful, transformative experiences of music-making for my students. These experiences involve building on and celebrating successes (our own and those of others), welcoming everyone regardless of background or ability, creating a positive and powerful sense of belonging, and never settling for less than musical excellence. I strive to develop habits of mind as much as habits of body by encouraging students to share individual and group ownership of the musical process and product. We make aesthetic choices and musical decisions together. I want my students to be able to *think* like musicians (not just do the behaviors musicians do). These are my priorities because they align closely with my core values about teaching and about children, as well as about music and music-making.

For many of my orchestra students, I am the sole architect of their experiences with and through music, so I want to make these meaningful. To plan, I begin with the end in mind. I believe that as a result of my instruction, students should become lifelong lovers and appreciators of music with the knowledge, skills, and motivation to participate in music for a lifetime. Since I seek to align all my actions with this, it has been important for me to analyze and unpack all of the implications of this for the following: what my actions and reactions should be in the classroom, the content of my activities, the broadness of my curriculum, and to what extent I need to connect with and teach *children* and not just teach music. Consider the words "lifelong lovers and appreciators." Wanting my students to be lifelong lovers and appreciators of music forces me to strive each day to be sure my rehearsals and classes are structured in positive, transformative, and meaningful ways that promote not just performance skills but also broad musical understandings in ways that help students become their own teachers and problem-solvers and make musical success and personal artistry possible.

Examining my own beliefs has helped me define my vision for what a successful program focused on individual student success looks like and feels like. This clarity has helped me to navigate small setbacks without losing heart by having the big picture in mind. It has also helped me take more joy in each small step of progress along the way, which has been my key for maintaining my positivity and passion over the years. I think every teacher should ask themselves the following questions:

- How do I *define* success? (now and in the future)

- Why do I believe orchestra *should be taught*? (Is this the same now as when I started?)
- What do I believe students *should know or be able to* do as a result of my instruction?
- In what *environment* do I believe music should be taught? (What am I doing or not doing to create this environment?)

Creating a short, bullet-pointed list of the answers to these questions (my own "Music Educator's Creed") continues to remind me who I am and what I am about as a teacher. When I see it over my desk, it helps guide and focus my planning of every rehearsal and musical experience. It has helped me to understand more clearly what I am trying to achieve in rehearsal (and in the program in general) and helps me communicate more clearly with students what is most important in our limited time together. In essence, I feel it helps me to make more of a difference in my students' lives than I would otherwise be able to make.

Rehearsal Preparation
Benjamin Franklin once said, "By failing to prepare, you are preparing to fail." Planning allows me to start all decision-making and problem solving from a much higher place and allows the spontaneity and freedom it takes to be successful in the moment. My most successful classes and rehearsal are those I've fully thought through and envisioned *from the student's perspective from beginning to end*, considering what would be effective, efficient, engaging, enjoyable, and motivating, and including easy access to all needed materials. I create a long-term and short-term plan based on my definition of what a great musician is and does and on the answers to the questions above. I try to have a clear, written, specific, achievable goal for each rehearsal as well as for each timed part of the rehearsal (warm-up, skill-building, and repertoire). I try to anticipate student difficulties in advance by playing through the parts on each instrument and looking for positive ways to overcome challenges as a group and as individuals.

I use an opening statement in each rehearsal to communicate both *what* we are working on as well as *why* it is important. Sharing goals each day with my students helps establish a clear sense of where we are going together in the rehearsal and how we can define success, and can help create a positive, forward momentum for each part of rehearsal. I try to avoid rehearsals that might feel like an exercise in error detection to my students (where students simply play until they make a mistake and then are told all the things they did wrong). As a musician (or human being), I can think of few things less gratifying or rewarding than this. I seek to balance detail work with play-through opportunities so I don't kill the joy of music-making for them and to remember that they are human beings who have not just musical but also psychological needs during the rehearsal. I recognize that the time I spend purposefully planning this balance can impact how much we achieve and how successful we feel about the work we do together.

I prepare for three areas of work in each rehearsal/class:

1. **Warm-up.** I teach for understanding and instrument mastery, not just performance. The warm-up for me is teaching time to introduce or reinforce the sequential skills, concepts, understandings, and "habits of mind" it takes to be a great musician. The warm-up is directly designed to introduce at least one clear, specific, and measurable goal that will be focused on during the parts of the class that follow it.

2. **Skill Building.** This is where the goal established in the warm-up (a specific technical skill or musical understanding) is practiced and refined so it can be applied to repertoire and to all future learning. This includes sequential work through a high-quality method book as well as exercises written by me. I follow a specific curriculum that covers state standards and my goals. I monitor progress using checklists for skill development in each of the following areas: pitch (scales, patterns), rhythms (simple to complex), bow exercises (tone and articulation work), sight-reading (separating pitch and rhythm skills), instrument-specific technical skills (such as extensions, shifting, etc.), and broad musical concepts (ensemble, listening, and appreciation skills). These are divided by unit and sequenced across grades 5–12 (or all grades in which orchestra is taught) and involve student "pass-offs" as they master each skill.

3. **Repertoire/Performance Preparation.** I spend a significant amount of time selecting repertoire that matches the level and needs of my students. The priority for me is that students be able to *make music with excellence* (not just play the notes and rhythms). Once pieces are selected, my process involves:

- **Score Study.** Listening, score analysis, marking the part with particular attention to form (thematic units), melodic tracing, dynamic/expression markings, cues, etc.
- **Rehearsal Map for Each Piece.** This is a rehearsal guide that breaks the piece up into teaching units. It includes a list of sections of the piece to be taught sequentially (related by form, skills/concepts, or measure numbers). Units are later divided up into weekly and daily plans and kept on file for future use.
- **Timeline.** I create an overall timeline to be sure I cover *all* measures of each piece well within the length of time and number of rehearsals I have. Specific goals and measures are laid out by unit of time associated with teaching each unit of each piece (addressing no more than one unit of each piece at a time).
- **Weekly and Daily Plans.** These are detailed plans made after reflecting on the previous rehearsal successes and challenges (often after listening to snippets I've recorded from the podium during rehearsal). My daily work plan includes:
  - *Goals* for the overall rehearsal to be stated in the warm-up as well as a specific goal for each piece we will work on. Piece goals are drawn from the units in the rehearsal maps for each piece and focus on mastering a musical skill (including a checklist of specific measure numbers and instruments to address).
  - *Strategies* for mastering skills and solving problems within the targeted measures (including warm-up activities and exercises that align with the curriculum goals and the goals of the repertoire).
  - *Timings* for pacing activities to balance work time and play-through time. I list the number of minutes ideally devoted to each section of rehearsal and adjust as needed. I keep a small clock on my podium to be sure I am not bogging down and killing all joy of music-making for my students.

Warm-Up

The warm-up is teaching time. Each day, I try to connect the warm-up to specific techniques or goals that will be addressed later in the rehearsal (and that align with the curriculum laid out in state and national standards). Work is heavily focused on skill development and making on sequential progress in each of the following four areas:

1. **Tone.** Open strings, bow hold, bowing, flexibility exercises, articulation work.
2. **Pitch.** Scales and exercises for intonation and pattern fluency work. Heavy emphasis on finger pattern and scale mastery.
3. **Rhythm.** Performing and recognizing rhythm patterns on open D within a sequential curriculum with focus on metronomic precision. After each set of rhythm patterns is mastered (pizz. while counting aloud and playing open D), it is combined with pitch-reading skills to practice sight-reading. We improvise and compose with these short rhythm and patterns to get better at sight-reading and to foster creativity as students find their voice to speak in the language of music.
4. **Technique.** Instrument-specific skills like shifting, extensions, spiccato, vibrato, etc.

Warm-up time includes stretching, working on healthy body alignment and proper instrument positioning to be sure that we are doing technical motions that are correct and tension-free with and without the instruments. Many motions are done first away from the instrument before being done on the instrument or bow. We break down technical skills such as (e.g., spiccato) and practice it in many different contexts from simplest to most complex: motions in the air away from the instrument, on open strings and with improvised patterns, on scales and familiar melodies, on exercises from the method book, and later on performance repertoire. I use a "sound before symbol" approach that emphasizes experience before labeling of sounds, patterns, and techniques (from the work of Pestalozzi and from Gordon Music Learning Theory pattern use). See "Additional Articles and Resources to Explore" at the end of this book for more details on Rolland, Pestalozzi, and Gordon.

Intonation and Fluency: Developing the Left Hand
My intonation work in the rehearsal is guided by these beliefs:

- Every student can play in tune given enough help.
- Poor intonation is unacceptable at any level.
- Having a group not be able to play in tune reflects more on me as a teacher than it does on my students. I must accept this to address it.
- Intonation instruction must be purposeful, sequential, and target both perception and execution skills to be successful.

- The more modalities I use in intonation instruction, the more successful students are. I use visual (finger patterns/spacing and fingerboard mapping/fingering charts), aural (ear training and diagnosis activities to promote audiation), and tactile-kinesthetic approaches (motor skill training and "target practice" for precision and adjustment, including exercises away from the instrument).
- Tuning time is time for structured intonation instruction: teaching students to recognize what it sounds like to be properly tuned and to be able to audiate pitches through sequential experience, teacher modeling, and active ear training. Perception and recognition both precede execution in ability development.
- Good intonation is not possible with poor left-hand position, and the order in which we introduce the use of fingers of the left hand can impact success. The importance of early instruction in the proper set-up of the left hand cannot be underestimated. Starting with fourth finger first encourages proper positioning of the elbow, hand, wrist, and fingers from the start. It also avoids later issues of pinky weakness and fear associated with using fourth finger. [See article "Fourth Finger First" in *American String Teacher Journal* (2015) Volume 65(2): 34–37.]
- Automaticity and independence must be developed for individual success. I teach students a sequence of set-up steps to chant and do in the same order every time we set the left hand to the instrument, reminding them repeatedly that "good musicians are not sloppy and they do not skip steps." I also reinforce the steps by posting them in the classroom and saying them aloud in the count-off routine. An ounce of prevention is worth a pound of nagging.

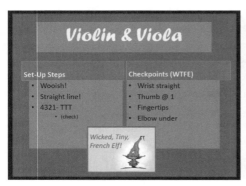

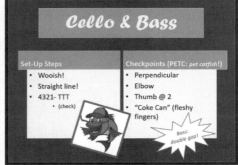

- Taking proactive positioning steps before playing results in less intonation nagging and correcting on the back end, which is more pleasant for everyone. Students need ways to independently self-assess their own positions.

Without an accurate mental image and clear understanding of half steps that combine with whole steps to make finger patterns, it is nearly impossible for string players to play in tune. It is imperative to play within a hand frame, not just note by note. I use finger pattern exercises and visuals to help students master the patterns below for upper strings and have low strings play along with corresponding notes on each string (being sure cellos keep equal spacing between fingers unless extended and that basses have twice as much space between the first and second fingers as other fingers).

Upper String Finger Patterns

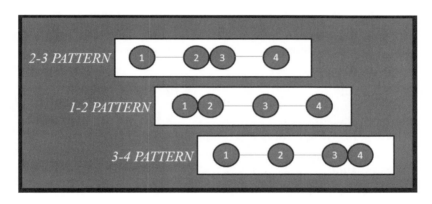

- It is important that students master each of the three distinct skills for each half/whole step pattern to play well in tune:
  - **Recognition.** Ability to recognize by ear and by feel when each pattern is in tune (first when someone else—like a teacher or another student—is playing, and then in themselves and their own playing).
  - **Execution.** Ability to physically execute the patterns with precise intonation and consistency (close enough half steps and wide enough whole steps).
  - **Application.** Ability to associate the patterns and pitch names with key signatures and specific musical repertoire. Students should be able to:

- complete fingering charts that map out the fingerboard (see Appendix B),
- say or sing correct pitch names while playing patterns, and
- determine which patterns to play according to the key signature of a piece and play them on each string.

Finger Pattern Instructional Sequence

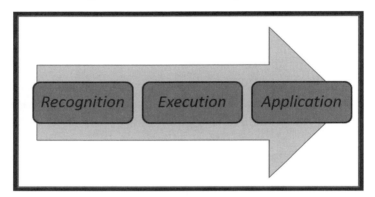

- It is helpful to learn advanced techniques that make intonation difficult away from the instrument and away from notation first. For example, the accurate finger spacing for cello extensions or bass fingering can be reinforced by having students touch their face with the following finger locations: pinky on the chin, third finger on the lower lip, second finger to top lip, and index finger pointed up to the eyebrow while curving the thumb at the middle finger. All violin and viola finger patterns can be done in the air away from the instrument or touched to circles drawn on index cards.
- Visual aids left on the instrument too long become crutches. Therefore, it is important to develop the ear, the aural image, and the finger dexterity skills simultaneously. Reliance should drift away from using the eyes to relying solely on the ears using sequential transition. Students must understand that the ear overrides the eye at all stages.
- Using external pitch reinforcement (accompaniment tracks from method books, drone, etc.) at home is essential. Without careful attention to tuning of the instrument (think electronic tuner or pitch producing device), students can reinforce bad intonation

68

habits for weeks and months at a time without consciously realizing it. Multiple research studies show that those who practice with accompaniment tend to play more in tune than those who do not.
- Playing with a relaxed hand frame in which each finger can be dropped easily into place without excess motion or rotation of the arm and wrist is crucial for intonation accuracy, as well as for later fluency, shifting, and vibrato.
- Ignoring is condoning. What I do not correct, my students seem to think I condone when it comes to poor intonation or poor left-hand technique, so just letting these go is not an option for me, no matter how tiresome it may be to correct them.

I understand that my own expectations and beliefs about intonation determine the extent to which I demand and facilitate excellence in this area. If I believe that even beginners can play in tune when given enough support and sequential instruction, they will. In addition, what I believe becomes internalized by my students and impacts their definition of "in tune" and thereby what they demand of themselves as success. Students will rise to the level of expectations. Any song too hard to play in tune is too hard for the student to play. Period.

Tone: Developing the Right Hand and Bow Control
String players paint their sound with their bows in much the same way that visual artists paint with a brush—by manipulating weight, speed, and contact point for expressive purposes in expressive combinations. Middle school is the perfect place to begin this artistic journey of teaching students to be expressive with and in control of their sound. I teach students the craft of manipulating each of these elements in concrete ways so they can later combine them in artistic and expressive ways. I incorporate a lot of modeling and listening because I believe that it is impossible for students to make a sound with their instruments that they do not first have in their ears and in their minds.

Here are a few ways I try to make the abstract ideas of tone production more concrete for my students:

- **Bow weight.** I talk about pounds of weight falling down on the string (0–100 pounds, coming through the arm and not by squeezing the hand). I ask students to make that "ugly" sound where the instrument barks at you because you pushed it too far (defining that sound as too far and never to be used, a "hundred pounder"). We apply various weights and describe each sound in words, then we vote on how much bow weight would sound best in specific sections of the repertoire. I let each class decide which numbers on the scale match each dynamic level or character through trial, discovery, and voting.

- **Bow Speed.** I talk in terms of driving the bow on the "highway" between the bridge and fingerboard at a controlled speed that is not reckless (especially at first). The speed should never be faster than students can control, keeping both the front tires and back tires in the same lane (straight bow) and without swerving across lanes and losing control of the vehicle. We establish five locations (or "lanes") between the bridge and fingerboard. Even inexperienced students can describe the difference in sound between driving the bow 100 miles per hour versus 10 miles per hour, and they can all theorize as to how speed can play a role in creating dynamics and notes that sound intense or angry versus relaxed and calm. We work on utilizing good bow distribution and keeping the angle straight by holding open D for varying lengths of time (16 beats then 8, 4, 2, and 1 without letting the sound die or get fuzzy at quarter = 60 on the metronome). I make students aware that the lower the instrument, the slower and heavier the bow weight needs to be to create the characteristic sound. Students don't naturally realize this, and basses sound terrible if they mirror the fast bow speeds of the violins.
- **Bow Contact Point.** Once we learn basics of placing the bow, I teach students to fight the habit of using a default placement (tip) or contact point (lane). Each time they start, they must consciously choose (and match with a stand partner). In class, we purposefully create an unusable and unacceptable sound (for example, bowing over the fingerboard) and label it as such. I train students to control the path of the bow first with highway lines drawn on an index card and threaded through the strings and then without. For beginners, the highway card has a single driving lane (made of two solid lines with one dotted line down the middle). In the second and third

years of orchestra, we graduate to an Atlanta-like "multi-lane high-way" with five lanes that all sound different (1 being by the bridge and 5 near the fingerboard). Students describe in words the differences in sound and practice using different lanes on open strings, scales, and familiar melodies. Thereafter, every time the bow is set on the string to play, we choose a lane. Putting the lane choice in the count-off is a good way to remind students ("lane-2-ready-go").

Stay in Your Lane

- **Part of the Bow.** An ensemble can only get a unified tone if everyone in the section is in the same part of the bow (frog, middle tip, upper half, lower half) using the same stroke. Students must learn to be aware of others and match their placements to unify sound. The warm-up is a great time to do follow-the-leader activities, as one student leader starts in one part of the bow and then changes to other parts while playing open strings or scales. We experiment with playing sections of the repertoire at different parts of the bow, diagnose the sound and feel, and then vote and mark it in the music. If students consistently have trouble playing at the frog, I have them turn the bow upside down to play for all or part of a rehearsal with the frog in front of the hand and the tip pointing to the right of the hand. This relaxes the upper part of the arm that controls the lower part of the bow.

A key element of consistent, characteristic tone production is awareness, so I ask students questions about what they are hearing and seeing from self and others, and for their input on what kind of sound they are seeking and how they can achieve it. For example: "How would this excerpt sound different in lane 2? Lane 5? With 80 pounds of weight? At the frog? What did you prefer? What gives us the character we think the music is calling for here? Can we vote as a group? Can we all mark it in the music?"

Many students struggle with tone for years due to faulty early set-up of the bow hand, tension in the bow hand, or lack of attentiveness to bow placement and angle from the earliest stages. Although I do grow weary of reinforcing and correcting these things, failing to do so can cripple students for a lifetime when it comes to beautiful tone production, since the hand and ear are constantly at war with each other. I try to find positive, fun, proactive, and creative ways to address technique on the front end with set-up steps, games, and exercises so that I can avoid so much nagging on the back end. One example is that I don't let any class use the bow to play arco until everyone in the group has a "Bowing Badge" or "License to Bow" that they can earn by demonstrating the correct bow hold on a pencil or straw.

Official SPPPI Bowing Badge

License to Bow!

I try to stay vigilant in planting and watering the seeds of good technique by looking for and reminding students of specific bow checkpoints—even if and when it falls on deaf ears. I might do this by saying things like, "If your thumb is curved and relaxed, good job."

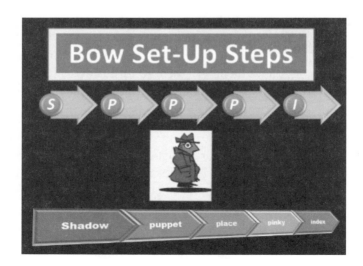

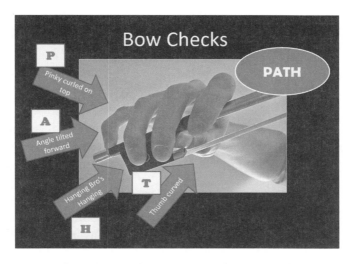

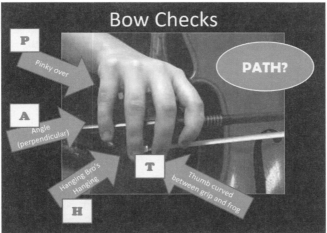

Tension is the enemy of good tone because it strangles the sound. I place tension-relieving exercises in the warm-up or create additional exercises on the fly throughout rehearsal to eliminate specific problems I see. For example, for straight pinky on the bow hand, I might ask violins and violas to tap their pinky fingernail on the bow stick, to create a click sound on every rest during a piece or scale.

Set-Up/Fundamentals: Instrument Position and Body Alignment
Technical excellence is a prerequisite for musical excellence. Automaticity and independence are key. This means students must become fully

automatic at the motions of setting up the instrument and body and given the tools to independently check and monitor themselves to know if they are doing it right or wrong. The importance of high expectations, creativity, and perseverance in helping students gain this automaticity and independence cannot be overestimated.

Musicians, like athletes, must learn to use our bodies correctly, naturally, and efficiently. Success depends on it, as does being able to play healthily over a lifetime. Tension in the body will create tension in the sound. Misalignment in the body (head, shoulders, hips, feet) will likely lead to pain, inefficient motion, or the inability to use the forces of gravity and physics to greatest advantage. When it comes to set-up, an ounce of prevention is worth more than a pound of nagging in my experience. The more time I spend getting students set-up properly at the start, the less time I generally spend nagging later. I have gotten my best results when I don't rush through the beginning stages of instruction to get to playing more difficult repertoire sooner. I think my job is to find a million ways to make musical excellence fun.

I use stretches, exercises, and learning proper motions away from the instrument first before applying motions to the instrument. Any motion that is difficult to do correctly away from the instrument will be more difficult to do correctly with the instrument. I teach my students a series of set-up steps with key words we chant for getting the instrument and body into the right playing position every time they play. Each step is designed to result in one correct checkpoint for instrument positioning. We often repeat the mantra, "Good musicians are not sloppy, and they do not skip steps." I find that doing each step correctly and incorrectly helps clarify what things should and should not look or feel like. Student are urged to use these at home, and I put posture reminder words into the count-offs in class. For example, I might give a three-bar count-off that sounds like this while snapping quarter notes, "Chair's Edge – –, Feet Flat – –, Spine-Aligned-Ready-Go." The less often I skip steps, the less often they will. I want my outer voice to become their inner voice for setting up.

If my students are still struggling with position after much instruction, I add fun games like "Position Charades" or "Position Physician," where students are shown pictures or videos of someone playing. Then I ask them to look at the instrument checkpoints and "diagnose" what ails the people pictured (or, if nothing is wrong, tell the person they should go home because they are a hypochondriac and don't need a doctor!).

Ensemble Playing: Unity, Precision, Tempo Stability
Getting students to play with passion, precision, and unity begins with habits of mind: attitude and awareness. True musicianship and high quality music-making require an attitude of being more willing to be together than to be right as well as the vigilance and focus to remain completely aware of others while playing. I ask my students to align everything about their playing both vertically (with the conductor) and horizontally (with each other).

Establishing a shared vision and identity as a group in which all members are willing to work together as a team towards common goals makes precision, unity, and good ensemble playing possible. I discuss with students the following questions: What is a great orchestra? What do great ensembles do that distinguish them from good ensembles? What kind of ensemble do we want to be? Having group buy-in and shared ownership of goals is crucial for the kind of motivation and effort that it takes to achieve true musical excellence. I ask my students to "play with passion, precision, and unity." Ensemble members communicate passion by bringing life, effort, attention, energy, and enthusiasm to rehearsals and focus on making musical meaning and not just playing notes and rhythms. This means that phrasing, articulation, and nuance are not things to be slapped on extra at the end. Playing within the correct character and emotion should occur from the start. Many notes and rhythms will fix themselves in the service of an artistic effort, but rarely will it go the other way around. An actor who is rehearsing an angry scene in a movie would never say the lines in any other way than angry (even if they miss a word or line of script). Expressiveness and passion are at the heart of why we do what we do, and to discount middle schoolers' abilities in this regard is to dehumanize them and the music they make. Passion alone, though, is not enough. Without precision and unity, results sound sloppy and chaotic because musicality cannot shine through muddy playing.

Students must learn the skill of becoming truly aware of others while playing. Each student must learn to lead, to follow, and to communicate without words. Musical awareness is a skill that can be taught reinforced every day, particularly the idea that it is more important to be together than to be right. The warm-up is a perfect time to release some control and autonomy to the ensemble to lead and follow each other and communicate without words. Each student must learn to do all three.

I post the following mantras in the classroom, and we repeat them often. During rehearsal when we are having trouble playing together, I often pause before the last word and have them fill in the blank:

- "It is more important to be together than to be ..." *"Right."*
- "Great musicians are ..." *"Team players."*
- "Teamwork means paying more attention to others than to ..." *"Myself."*

To get students to play with unity and precision, I try to gamify the work. With even the youngest students, unifying tempo, bowings, bow placement, cutoffs, entrances, and dynamics can be practiced on open strings in a game I call "Don't Get Tricked." In this game, all students begin playing open D quarter notes together and then follow a chosen leader. For older students, a "Unity Warm-up" includes aligning: part of the bow (frog, middle, tip), bow direction (often going in the same direction multiple times), bow stroke (staccato, spiccato, legato, etc.), contact point (bridge, fingerboard, etc.), and phrasing by leaning on selected important notes within groups of four. I also try to unify starting breaths before every entrance (within and across sections). Even within stands, at a very basic level, if you cannot match strokes and be exactly together with your stand partner, you likely can't do it across the orchestra. Partners pledging to follow each other and be together always goes a long way. Unifying the inner circle of confident, principal players is also helpful because sometimes it is the stubborn and confident section leader that drags the ensemble apart as much as the reluctant or dragging players who are not confident in making the entrances.

When it comes to tempo control, I have found that there is absolutely no trick, game, or substitute that can take the place of consistent and methodical use of a metronome as an ensemble, combined with vigilant counting and subdividing by students.

When having students subdivide quarter notes with "1 & 2 & 3 & 4 &" doesn't work, I have them say or sing out loud other words like: "1 – wait – 2 – wait – 3 – wait – 4 – wait" or "lizard, lizard, lizard, lizard" or "cello, cello, cello, cello" (if cellos have eighth notes that they should follow), or "tick-tock, tick-tock, tick-tock, tick-tock" (if pizzicato must be as steady as a clock). It's also fun to use the name of the student everyone should be following ("Amy, Amy, Amy, Amy"). Also, saying "me – them – me – them – me – them – me – them" helps students to align with another section's subdivisions by reminding them how they fit into the big picture. This reminds them that they have to wait for others. Rhythmic precision is the foundation on which musical expression and excellence is built. Without precise alignment even the best phrasing, subito dynamic, or expressive elements will not be heard clearly.

Finding new and better strategies to get my students to play with passion, precision, and unity by encouraging awareness, positive attitudes, and a sense of community and belonging remain lifelong goals for me in my work with orchestras. Having students learn to communicate without words, to be aware of others, and to respond to and follow others creates the kind of bond in music-making experiences that allow students to make memories that last a lifetime.

Expression: Phrasing, Balance, Dynamic Contrast

At its most basic level, phrasing is about helping students find where the most and least important notes are in each part of the music and determining which notes should be grouped together. The simplest, most obvious way I've found to communicate this to middle schoolers is to liken it to language. Words in a sentence are as notes in a phrase. It not only matters *what* words we say but also *how* we say them that communicates meaning. Just like actors who are given a script, we must decide how to say the words (notes) to convey meaning, deciding which words require more emphasis because they are more important (generally spoken more strongly or loudly) and which ones should trail away because they are less important (generally spoken more gently or softly).

I teach students how to bring reasonable, subtle emphasis to important notes and to trail away on others by using expression exercises and games and by modeling choices. I have them practice manipulating specific bow weights and bow speeds to lean towards certain notes and to trail off on others. In follow-the-leader games, I ask them to recognize the expression of others (and me) as we play open D. Different leaders take turns leaning towards one of the notes in a group of four. In this way, we practice both execution and awareness skills. We do the same activities on simple, well-known melodies, and I ask them what notes they prefer as a class in our concert repertoire. I make it clear to students that they should always be looking for and leaning on the most important note in each phrase and noticing which notes their stand partners and sections are leaning on in order to unify without the conductor always spelling it out. In this way, one ensemble interpretation of a piece is being negotiated constantly—without words—between members of the ensemble and in response to conducted patterns.

With regard to balance, it is hard for young students to understand that if everyone has *forte*, everyone cannot play *forte* or the melody will not be heard. Those with the melody will have to play a little louder and those without it, softer. The issue is how much softer or louder? I try to make it simple and concrete for students. For example, if I have eight violas on the melody and forty-eight others in the rest of the ensemble, I might pair up one violist with six other people and ask others if they can still hear the melody, making it clear that every six people must be softer than one person in the viola section. To avoid frustration, I try to provide help by saying things like:

- "That sounded like about 80 pounds of bow weight; can we try 15?"
- "That sounded like an 8 on the volume knob; can you make it a 3?"
- "That looked like 100 mph of bow speed; can you try 30 and see what it sounds like?"

I raise awareness of balance by playing games like "Spotlight." In this game, each section stands up and plays only when they have the melody; otherwise they are seated and silent (but expected not to get lost). This is an active and visible way for everyone to hash out together where the melodies are and how to recognize them. We mark the name of the section that is "speaking" in our parts at each rehearsal number so that others do not "talk" over them "rudely."

I liken dynamics in music to how volume level is used in speech to communicate emotion. Shouting means something very different emotionally than whispering. Middle school students love drama, so we map out the drama or emotion of the piece through the dynamic levels by posing questions like: "If this were a movie scene, what would be going on?" or "What story, scenes, or key words would this class attach to each section in this piece if we created an expression map?" and then, "How can we use our bows physically to create these sounds and communicate each word you chose?" I also have students play entire pieces with a game of "Sit, Stand, Crouch" to force them to locate all the dynamic changes in a whole piece quickly. They are forced to make dynamic decisions and changes quickly enough as their section sits for *piano*, crouches for medium dynamics, and stands for loud dynamics, all exactly together. Crescendos should gradually stand together and decrescendos gradually sit, which can be very helpful in pacing the decay or increase of these over time.

Articulation Control

I liken articulation of notes to enunciating words in speech to help students understand that it is an expressive tool, not just something to do without understanding because the director told you to. I have had little success getting students to consistently buy in to a single unified articulation if they do not understand *why* the articulation is needed. I ask questions like, "What character are we trying to create here?" Just like in human speech, how smoothly we say certain words makes a big difference in the meaning others perceive. Modeling several articulation options for students or explaining a particular bow stroke choice (and modeling it) can bring an artistic and creative element to an otherwise mundane rehearsal of note and rhythm learning. It is never too early to begin this work. Even beginning fifth graders can try to use their bow to create "Mary Had an Angry Lamb" or "Mary Had a Lonely Lamb." To ignore articulation until the end of the learning instead of as part of the process of repetition in music learning means ignoring opportunities for enjoyment, appreciation, and music-making along the way. To me, this is essential, not extra, because notes and rhythms are not enough, and survival (just reaching the end of a piece without falling apart) is not a musical goal—although I know we have all been thankful for simple survival sometimes!

Together, we work to master the craft of articulation so that later the art can come. We work on specifics of exactly how to manipulate the bow weight, speed, contact point, and part of the bow to get the different articulations, which creates the different characters, emotions, and moods in music. Unified interpretation means that everyone within the ensemble (not just the front of the section) must be able to lead and follow others to match motion. Motions can be learned and reinforced away from the instruments in the air as well. For example, draw a smile in the air with your bow for spiccato strokes, draw a Nike swoosh for detaché, touch the hot stove and back away for accents, spread the peanut butter for legato, or pet the kitty for a slightly separated but gentle louré.

Repertoire

Selecting repertoire is one of the most important decisions that directors make. Well-chosen repertoire leads to energizing, engaged, successful rehearsals and music-making. Poorly selected repertoire can lead to boredom, frustration, lack of success, low engagement, behavior issues, mediocre or poor performances, and even worse: student internalization of low standards for music-making or lack of desire to continue playing. Choices determine if the average rehearsal will feel mostly negative (with the orchestra crashing and burning as the piece falls apart multiple times) or mostly positive and gratifying (as the ensemble makes progress because there is a realistic balance of difficulty and ease that enables actual music-making).

Excellence is impossible if the repertoire is too difficult to play musically with expression. As orchestra directors, we write our students' internal definitions of musical excellence by what we accept in rehearsal and so we should not accept mediocrity. We must select repertoire realistically for the group we have in front of us, not for the group we want or wish we had. With training and patience, we can build skills to master more difficult repertoire. If we have to err to one side, I find it far better to pick music that is a little too easy than too difficult because with easier music, students can play musically and in tune, and once mastered, you can always add pieces to a concert program. It can be, however, very demoralizing and demotivating to take pieces away from students or to have students fail in public performance. In addition, students will sacrifice good technique when playing repertoire that is too difficult too soon. Although, there are many things that I take into consideration when selecting repertoire, none of them are more important than the students themselves and what kind of experience they will have with the music.

Here are a few of my favorite pieces (for right now):

Easy
- "Cinnamon" or "Soul Strings" from *Stringing Along, Volume 1* by Stoutamire and Henderson. If you can only get one thing other than a method book for your beginners, get this! It's a must-have.
- "Canyon Sunset, by John Caponegro.
- "Moonlight Tango," by Richard Meyer (or almost anything by this composer).
- "Tribal Dance," by Brian Balmages (or almost anything by this composer).

Intermediate
- "Gauntlet," by Doug Spata (or almost anything by this composer) "El Toro," by Don Brubaker.
- "St. Anthony Chorale," by Haydn/Sandra Dackow (or almost any classic by this arranger).
- "Danse Infernale," by Elliot Del Borgo (or almost any quick tempo piece by this composer).

Advanced
- "Arabian Dreams," by Soon Hee Newbold (or almost anything by this composer).
- "Lullaby," by William Hofeldt (or almost any slow piece by this composer).
- "Legend," by David O'Fallon.
- "1812" Overture, by Tchaikovsky/ arr. Dackow.

Recruiting/Community Building
The heart and soul of recruiting is giving students the highest quality musical experience that you can every single day that they enter your classroom. No amount of salesmanship or flashy recruiting can sell a product not worth buying. That is not to underestimate the power or worth of

high-quality elementary recruiting performances and materials (one of the most important performances of the year for your program), but the reasons people join and continue to stay in a program have more to do with how positive and transformative the experiences are all year long. A program built around people, relationships, and high-quality music-making and founded on the ideas of community, shared ownership, and musical excellence sells itself when done well. Here are a few strategies that I have found to be most successful over the years:

- **Students Recruiting Other Students.** I start a recruiting wall of fame for each section on the front wall of the classroom, and each time someone recruits a sibling, friend, or neighborhood acquaintance, we add their name to the wall under that section.
- **Myth Busting.** I intentionally spell out these myths and actively combat them in elementary recruiting concerts, making the case that orchestra is for everyone. Some of these common myths and ways to combat them are below:
  - *Instruments and Gender:* There are no boy instruments or girl instruments!
  - *Identity Groups:* All types of people are welcome. Orchestra is for everyone. We have athletes, cheerleaders, chess club members, drama club members, as well as people of all different backgrounds and ethnicities.
  - *Scheduling:* You don't have to give up sports, advanced classes, or other activities to be in orchestra. (Demonstrate how it is possible to participate in more than one group. Consider having a sample schedule ready to show.)
  - *Costly*: Explicitly state that no one will be denied this once-in-a-lifetime opportunity because of finances. Tell students, "If you need help, let me know. We'd love to have you with us."
  - *Not "Cool":* Show how orchestral instruments are everywhere in life—movies, TV, radio, cartoons, etc.—and show students that they can play all different styles of music.
  - *Previous Skill/Knowledge:* Explain that absolutely no prior experience or knowledge is necessary. "You do not have to read music to join. We will even teach you how to take it out of the case."
  - *Difficulty:* Show how it is easy to start plucking from day 1 by bringing someone up from the audience who has never played

before and inviting them to pluck open strings on a cello while you play a melody over them. (Think *Star Wars* or *The Pink Panther* or something even cooler.) One of your cellists can help make sure the instrument doesn't slide away, and the audience can participate with clapping, snapping, or sound effects.

- **Proactive Registration Measures.** I have everyone in the fourth grade complete the orchestra registration form to with yes or no to joining. This choice architecture has been huge for me in getting more students enrolled and making sure registration forms get to parents. I offer teacher prizes and class prizes to the homeroom who gets all their forms in first.

- **High-Quality Recruiting Concert and Materials.** This concert must sound good, look good, and make orchestra seem to be the best thing since sliced bread. If you want them to be convinced that orchestra is fun, then this concert should prove it. I recognize and give laminated "VIP" passes to my current elementary fifth grade students who play so they can sit in the front row and meet high school performers after the show.

- **Connecting Schools.** I take eighth graders on a field trip to the high school during the school day for orientation and to rehearse and perform side-by-side each February. I take elementary students to the middle school to play their pieces in the middle school orchestra room and to tour the school. Each year, the final spring concert is a pyramid concert of the students and parents can see the full progression of fifth graders through high school seniors. In addition, they can see seniors who have stayed enrolled in the program for eight years being recognized, and they all perform a grand finale piece together. For a full description of this, see "An Innovative Idea for Building Community and Program-Wide Support through Creative Programming of a Spring Concert Grand Finale Tradition" in *The Conductors Companion: 100 Rehearsal Techniques, Imaginative Ideas, Quotes and Facts* by Sandy Goldie (edited by Gary Stith and published by Meredith Music Publications).

Rebecca MacLeod

> "It took me a long time to come to the conclusion that talent is not what is important. Persistence, grit, and determination is what leads people to success over time."

Dr. Rebecca MacLeod *is associate professor of music education at the University of North Carolina at Greensboro, specializing in string education. She earned her degrees from Duquesne University (BSME) and Florida State University (MME and PhD). Prior to her position at UNCG, she taught elementary, middle school, and high school orchestra in the public schools of Pennsylvania. Her research on working with underserved populations, vibrato technique, teacher effectiveness, and music perception has been presented nationally and internationally. She is a sought-after guest conductor and clinician throughout the United Sates.*

Rehearsal Philosophy
I have three guidelines when rehearsing:

- Success breeds success.
- Students need to be empowered.
- We need to teach persistence.

Rehearsals go well when ensemble members feel successful the majority of the time, particularly in middle school. Beginning the rehearsal with something that allows students to be successful and musical is essential.

The energy profile that Bob Culver presents in his *Master Teacher Profile* outlines a beautiful model for engaging rehearsals. Begin with review, then move the rehearsal into a place where students have the opportunity to work on something challenging. The end of rehearsal should be fast paced, provide closure, and be motivating so that the students want to return.

Students who are empowered to be independent are more likely to become lifelong learners and participators in music. Independence has to be cultivated by teaching students how to practice, how to navigate challenges, and how to use a variety of tools to overcome those challenges. For example, they need to be able to learn difficult passages. In rehearsal, I like to isolate a passage and show students how I would break it down to learn it myself. We do these steps together as a group, then I choose another passage and ask them to apply the same steps on their own while I watch them. We take a few minutes in rehearsals for them to dissect a passage, and I observe, choosing students who are successful to explain the process that they used to learn the passage to others. Using student leaders rather than the teacher to demonstrate or explain can be much more powerful than always having the teacher provide the answer. Students can relate to their peers and often feel that they can do it if one of their friends can do it.

Finally, we teach persistence. Choosing repertoire that is only slightly out of students' reach will motivate them to work towards that goal. If the target is too close or too far, students will generally give up. There is a threshold that the teacher or conductor can sense during a rehearsal when students are becoming frustrated. Rather than avoiding that feeling of frustration altogether, it is important to approach the threshold so that students' capacity to persevere is increased. If you always avoid the threshold, students may never reach their full potential. However, teachers need to be aware of when the threshold has been passed because students have trouble recovering after they are pushed too far. Life is filled with challenges. Try to teach students how to overcome challenges so that when they are faced with them in life, they have some tools to persevere.

Rehearsal Preparation
Part of preparing for rehearsal is choosing appropriate music. I spend an incredible amount of time choosing repertoire and thinking about how my

students will benefit from each piece. In many cases, I will arrange something specifically for them so that I can differentiate the learning for each person in the class. I do this for my elementary students as well as for my university students, constantly making adaptations so that everyone can feel successful and included. I want to teach students good executive skills and musicianship skills and provide opportunities for creativity, which is most easily done when music is at the appropriate level.

Once the music has been selected, the value of rehearsal preparation cannot be overestimated. I can still vividly recall the first rehearsal that I conducted where I truly knew the score. I had always admired conductors who could seemingly hear everything. While I was in graduate school, I attended a conducting workshop in Chicago hosted by the American Symphony Orchestra League. The professional conductors leading this workshop suggested that a conductor should spend three hours on score study for every minute of music *prior to standing on the podium.* I put that equation to the test in my own personal study and found that I could suddenly hear things that I hadn't previously considered. Not only that, but my mind was free to really focus on the musicians in front of me during rehearsal because I already knew what I was expecting to hear and could compare it to what I was actually hearing. It does not take the same amount of time for me to learn a grade 1–4 piece as it does for me to learn a Beethoven symphony. Nevertheless, the basic principle does apply. When teachers know their music well, they teach better.

After attending that workshop, I adopted a fairly standard approach to learning musical scores. Initially, I listen to as many great performances of the piece that I can find. Once I begin studying the piece, I will put the recordings away and rely on my inner hearing to learn the piece. I generally create a score graph that outlines the phrasing, and I analyze the harmony at the start and finish of phrases. I also make sure to choose a performance tempo that I stick to consistently. I write that number at the top of my score, then practice audiating the score using a metronome set to the tempo I intend to use in performance. While I am learning the score, I will also do bowings. I usually end up using both a piano and my violin during my score study process.

Once I know the score well, I am ready to begin making a rehearsal plan. I first look for transferable moments in the score so that I can teach conceptually; this also allows students to think conceptually and become more independent. For example, if I am teaching the orchestra how to play with a legato sustained sound, I will first present this concept in the warm-up. Once the group has achieved a legato sound, I will ask the students to locate passages in their music that use the same style and reinforce the concept throughout the repertoire.

I usually include a warm-up at the start of a rehearsal with younger students. Warm-ups are designed to either teach a concept (such as beautiful tone) or to teach a technical skill (such as cello extensions). Dr. Michael Allen, my former mentor, used to characterize warm-ups as either pre-determined routines or interactive activities. I tend to lean towards using interactive warm-ups that change every day and are directly related to the instructional goals for that rehearsal. Interactive warm-ups are frequently rote activities where the teacher or a student leader models a technique or musical idea and the other students respond. This type of warm-up eliminates the visual element of reading music and fully engages students' ears. It also allows students to focus on their technique. Pre-set routines can be excellent for focusing students but sometimes lead to students going through the motions without carefully attending to their personal technique or using their ears. Interactive warm-ups force students to watch and listen in order to participate.

Intonation and Fluency: Developing the Left Hand
Left-hand facility is predicated on good instrument position that allows the left hand to be flexible and balanced. When I assess students' left hands, I tend to regard the student's entire set-up because many issues with the left hand actually originate in the relationship between the body and the instrument. The most common elements that I look for across the four bowed instruments are: straight wrist, boxed fingers, and relaxed thumb. For violins and violas, I always check that the left-hand fingernails face the low string side of the students' bridge (in other words, for violins, the fingernails should be facing their bridge towards the G string). Cellists' and bassists' fingernails should face the nearest adjacent string.

Playing descending scales helps reinforce a good left-hand frame with fingers that hover close to the fingerboard and good left-hand spacing for intonation. Students who can identify octaves, half steps, and whole steps tend to be able to play more in tune. Finger patterns are also very beneficial in getting students to prepare their left hand. For violins and violas, understanding that half steps involve fingers that nearly touch is essential. Developing cellists need to spend time planning when to execute extensions and how to plan ahead so that the second finger has moved to its proper location before they attempt to use the fourth finger. Finally, bass players should focus on maintaining a K-position in their left hand where there is a half step between their first and second fingers, and another half step between their second and fourth fingers. An awareness of whether they are shifting the distance of a half step or whole step will also greatly increase their accuracy.

While shifting is frequently thought of as an intermediate technique, I think it should be taught almost immediately in the form of pre-shifting activities and games. Playing a scale and tapping the left hand on the right shoulder between each pitch helps ensure that the instrument is supported by the body position and not the left hand. Pinky pizzicato and shuttle games that involve plucking the string from first position to very high positions are good starting exercises. Once students left hands are mobile, I will introduce the halfway harmonics and begin having students play sirens (slide the left hand) and ghost tremolos (using a tremolo bow and sliding the left hand without compressing the string so that harmonics are played).

In a heterogeneous string class, I introduce landmark positions—those positions that correspond to an open string (positions I, III, IV, and VII). These positions allow students to double check the accuracy of their pitch with the open string. Many players and teachers do not realize that everyone's (violin, viola, cello, and bass) third position is a perfect fourth above the open string. Likewise, everyone's fourth position is an open fifth above the open string. This homogeneity in how fingerboard geography is constructed is very useful for the heterogeneous string class.

Tone: Developing the Right Hand and Bow Control
Good tone starts with a good bow hold that is flexible. I look for the following basic checkpoints in students' bow holds: stick of the bow

one-and-a-half knuckles deep, thumb bent, and flexible fingers. For violin and viola players, I also check that they are pronating their hand (leaning towards their index finger) and have the pinky perched on top of the bow. For cello and bass players, I check that their hand is square and their pinkies are one pad deep. I recommend daily flexibility exercises from Paul Rolland's *Teaching of Action in String Playing*.

Bow arm mechanics allow students to control the bow and keep it parallel to the bridge. Partner activities with dowel rods and PVC piping can assist students in achieving a bow that moves parallel to the bridge. In middle school, it is important to revisit this motion because students are continuing to grow. As their bodies change, so does their relationship with the instrument.

In terms of developing a beautiful sound, I recommend that students work hard to get a consistent bow speed before trying to use different articulations. Consistent speed is difficult and requires students to plan out their bow distribution. The same is true for consistent weight. If students can draw the bow parallel to the bridge with consistent speed and consistent weight with the bow halfway between the bridge and fingerboard, then I will begin to introduce different articulations in this order: **martelé**, collé, slurs, hooked bows, and off the string.

Set-Up/Fundamentals: Instrument Position and Body Alignment
Fundamentals never go away. Younger students can easily tire of going over the basics. I try to use the analogy of physical exercise as a way of thinking about technique. No one would say, "Well I exercised yesterday, so I accomplished that and I don't need to do that ever again." Exercise is a lifelong activity just as is playing open strings, working on flexibility, or intonation. With this in mind, students should regularly review their fundamentals.

I look for the following in basic body position and alignment:

Violin and Viola
- Feet should be hip-width apart with weight evenly balanced between both legs.
- The violin/viola rests on the student's shoulder. Use a shoulder rest, sponge, or raised chin rest to decrease the distance between the jaw and the chin rest so that the student's head remains aligned and comfortable.

- The end button of the violin/viola should be slightly to the left of the center of student's neck.
- Students should be able to hold the violin without their hands for limited amounts of time.
- The jaw rests on the chin rest and the student's head should favor the left ear.
- The violin/viola should be parallel to the floor.

Cello

- The student's upper legs should create a 90-degree angle to the floor. The placement of the feet is determined by the height of the student. Taller students may need to move their feet closer to the chair so that their upper legs are at a 90-degree angle to the floor.
- The endpin and feet make an equilateral triangle.
- The heel of the neck of the cello should fall approximately over the student's heart.
- The lower bouts of the cello should be knee level.
- The C-peg should go behind the student's left ear.

Bass

- The bass height should allow the student's right hand to reach the bridge, first finger of the left hand in first position is at eye level. If there is a big difference between these checkpoints in terms of left and right hand, then the bass is likely too large and the student would benefit from an instrument that is smaller.
- Standing Position: Feet should be shoulder-length apart, flat on the floor, and relaxed, with the left foot just slightly forward and turned out.
- Seated Position: The player should rest on the stool with the right foot flat on the floor and the left foot on the first rung of the stool.
- The bass must be supported by the left hip bone.
- The right lower bout comes in slight contact with the inside of the left knee.
- Students should be able to balance the bass with no hands or let the instrument fall slightly forward.

Ensemble Playing: Unity, Precision, Tempo Stability

Human beings have difficulty sensing the passing of time. This is why we need to use timekeeping devices to know what time of day it is. For this reason, working daily on steady pulse is so important. Students and teachers alike need to work regularly with a metronome, matching an external pulse, then internalizing that pulse. Both skills are important for ensemble unity. I like to include regular metronome practice with my ensembles using a variety of strategies.

One of my favorite activities is a metronome game where students count from one to eight with a metronome on. Then I turn the sound off, and they continue to count. Generally, when I turn the sound back on (approximately eight to ten beats later), they have drifted from the original tempo. We continue this game with them counting out loud, then inside their minds, then out loud, until they are able to count together and stay with the metronome. Another favorite activity is to have them play the subdivision of a melodic passage. In other words, they play constant sixteenth notes with their bow while changing pitch at the correct moment so that the melody is recognizable. I also have my ensembles perform with a human metronome. For this activity, half of the orchestra subdivides constant sixteenth notes on the tonic while another section of the orchestra performs their passage in time with the sixteenth notes. These activities develop students' ability to subdivide and listen to others in the ensemble and help students internalize the pulse.

Another aspect of precision is matching bow strokes and bow placement. Teaching students to match their principal player from early in the orchestral experience is important. If students subdivide, listen, and match note lengths, they will sound much more together and have excellent ensemble skills.

Expression: Phrasing, Balance, Dynamic Contrast
Like shifting, expressive playing can be taught early on but should not interfere with students having good instrument position, good tone, precise rhythm, and accurate intonation. Playing expressively includes these foundational elements. Playing with a wide variety of dynamics with wrong notes and wrong rhythms is neither musical or expressive. Having said that, humans are innately musical, and young students can be very expressive when given the opportunity and can play both accurately and expressively.

In middle school, phrasing is taught best through dynamics that follow the melodic contour, overall style that stays consistent, and moments of rubato. Students need to grasp how to play with different dynamics. At a basic level, this can be achieved by teaching them to change their contact point: away from the bridge is softer, closer to the bridge is louder. Ultimately, they may also be able to achieve different colors and dynamics by varying their bow speed. Nothing is more beautiful, however, than listening to and watching a middle school orchestra that can change tempo as an ensemble. I try to teach students to watch and stretch notes as early as I believe they are able. Teaching students to slow down is much more difficult than teaching them to speed up. This is why we need to spend even more time teaching them to slow down.

Articulation Control

I am a firm believer in teaching students to use consistent bow speed before introducing a variety of articulations. Once students can produce a beautiful tone using consistent speed and weight while bowing parallel to the bridge, I then introduce the martelé bow stroke. The start to the martelé bow stroke grips the string, the bow moves quickly, then it stops and remains on the string. Executing this bow stroke for maximum resonance builds a foundation for all of the other on-the-string articulations.

Legato is one of the most difficult bowing styles for young students. Creating a seamless sound during a bow change is challenging and requires a balanced, flexible bow hold. Additionally, students must learn to slow the bow down during the bow change rather than speeding it up, which is their natural tendency when changing direction. Games that encourage students to play with a circular or endless tone can help them smooth out their bow changes and achieve a legato bow stroke.

Teaching off-the-string playing to young students seems difficult, yet the natural tendency of bow is to bounce. In some ways, we make bouncing difficult because we begin bouncing after we have learned to keep the bow on the string. Exploring the balance point and bouncing silently in earlier instruction can encourage students to bounce. While many students think that bouncing is difficult, I actually think the real problem is in keeping a consistent tone while bouncing. In my experience, students can bounce, but it sounds very percussive. To get more tone, I teach them to use a brush stroke first and encourage them to use more horizontal motion. I also have students practice bouncing by holding their bows at the balance point. This relieves tension in the hand, gives them more control, and allows them to hear the more resonant sound that they are trying to achieve. If they have an aural picture, they almost always are more successful.

Repertoire

I talked about repertoire in terms of preparing for rehearsal. When I choose repertoire, I primarily think about my students and what I want to teach them. This includes both musical and technical goals. If I want to introduce shifting, I may choose a piece that includes harmonics and simple shifts. If I think that students need more experience counting in groups of three, I may choose something in 6/8. Recently, I have been attempting to include more opportunities for improvisation in my orchestra classes.

Some of my favorite pieces for middle school orchestra, grades 2–3, include:

- "Iowa Spring," by Paul Seitz
- "Canyon Sunset," by John Caponegro
- "Three Tunes from Shakespeare," by Nicholas Hare
- "Westminster Prelude and Fugue," by David Shaffer
- "Tam Lyn," by Bob Phillips and Crystal Plohman
- "Declarations," by Jeffrey Bishop
- "Danza," by Vaclav Nehlybel
- "M to the Third Power," by Carold Nunez
- "Déjà vu," by Carold Nunez
- "Symphony No. 1," by William Boyce, arr. Folus

Recruiting/Community Building

Building a strong orchestra program involves more than what happens in the classroom. Teachers who are really successful in building strong programs understand the students and families that are part of the community in which they work. I recommend becoming part of that community. Get to know both students and families in your district.

Equally important is that students know and trust one another. I strongly recommend incorporating social activities into the curriculum. These can occur within or outside the classroom. Building relationships between students and families will also create a community that supports the arts in the schools.

Use near peers as frequently as possible when recruiting. Students really look up to slightly older peers. As distance in age increases, students sometimes relate less—or at least differently—to the older person. Sometimes the distance in age is positive, but certainly the relationship is different. Older peers can really influence younger students to join and continue being involved in music (or other activities).

Finally, I recommend engaging students in musical activities when attempting to recruit. Allowing students to experience music-making can be very powerful. The excitement and joy on their faces as they play a musical instrument for the first time is irreplaceable. Recruiting with interactive music-making is very effective. Students tend to be much more engaged if the music is approachable for them and if they can participate. We frequently think that something flashy or difficult may compel students to join, but they really are most excited when they think that they are able to do whatever it is that the teacher is showing them.

Anne Marie Patterson

> "My motto: Make it easy for students to learn, make it fun so they will want to!"

Anne Marie Patterson *holds a bachelor's degree in music performance from Washington and Lee University and a master's degree in perfor- mance and music education from Florida State University. She has been a freelance violinist in the Washington, D.C. area for seventeen years, and has performed with Midori, Sarah Chang, Leonard Slatkin, Branford Marsalis, Richard Stolzman, and many others. She served as president of the MD/DC chapter of the American String Teachers Association, and has been a presenter at the National ASTA Convention. She currently teaches at Theodore G. Davis Middle School in Charles County, Maryland and directs the Charles County Youth Orchestra and Encore Strings.*

Rehearsal Philosophy

I believe that every rehearsal should maximize student progress. That may seem like an obvious goal, but it is extremely difficult to accomplish. You must establish effective procedures for seating, tuning, passing out materi- als, and all of the other potential time-wasters that are inevitable realities in the music classroom. I always tell students, "You get good at what you do a lot." Therefore, it's important to play as much as possible. Every rehearsal needs to reinforce good position and technique while gradually introducing students to increasingly more complicated rhythms, finger pat- terns, and bowing techniques. Some students will grasp concepts easily, some will struggle, but the vast majority should be kept at the edge of their ability in order to maintain challenge and maximize interest. If you can add elements of fun and camaraderie to this staggering list of challenges, you are likely a genius and sure to have a successful string program!

Rehearsal Preparation

Preparing for rehearsals should take place on the macro as well as micro level. Before the school year begins, plan your goals for each grade level. Beginning classes will start with instrument position, basic technique, and note reading, and may get as far as "low 2s," (F natural for example), G-string notes, slurs, and hooked bows. Advanced classes may begin with an assessment to determine their current skill level and work toward improving fluency, intonation, vibrato, third position, complicated rhythms, etc. (Consult the ASTA String Curriculum or the curriculum for your area.)

Within the structure of the year's goals, each class should begin with warm-ups, scales, and technical exercises, then move to a method book and/or rehearsal of music that is appropriate for their grade level. I use a lesson planner to record what I have done with each daily class in order to remember where to start next time. I note difficulties students are having as well as reminders to prepare specific materials for upcoming classes. It is extremely valuable to keep these records from year to year so I can be sure I'm introducing material in a timely fashion, remembering all my good ideas, and moving on from the unsuccessful ones.

Warm-Up

It is important to have a variety of effective warm-up strategies. This is the first thing the class will do for the day, so it is important to establish and reinforce good technical habits while creating an inviting, engaging environment. All classes, from beginning to advanced, will benefit from Paul Rolland–style movement exercises: slide on the fingerboard, tap in high position (at the harmonic spot), left pinky strum, etc. Scales themselves are important for learning key signatures and finger patterns, but they can also be used to practice a variety of bowing techniques such as **martelé**, spiccato, and bow distribution. In my advanced classes, I let students take turns directing the scales, implementing bowing techniques I draw from their repertoire. I also teach familiar melodies by rote to practice finger patterns, especially anything chromatic, like the theme from *Batman*. Other concepts to work into warm-up time are dynamics, vibrato, rhythms, articulation, breathing, movement, and following the conductor. Try to incorporate games into your very practical and technical warm-ups so that students think they're just having fun.

Intonation and Fluency: Developing the Left Hand
Intonation is dependent upon good technique, and all left-hand technique is dependent upon correct instrument placement. (See section on instrument position.) Once basic position has been established correctly, students on all instruments should slide and tap on the fingerboard to establish balance and ease of motion and to prepare for shifting. Be sure to tap the thumb, as it is often a culprit for tension. Cello and bass players maintain a C shape in their hand, avoiding any collapse of the finger joints. Their thumb should be centered on the back of the neck. Do not let the thumb slide to the side of the neck or point up toward the scroll. Violin and viola players create a tighter C shape by making a hook shape with the fingers (square knuckles) but keeping the base knuckles relatively flat. Beginning violin/viola players should practice using the fourth finger right away so they get used to bringing the base knuckles close to the fingerboard to achieve a round pinky shape. The ideal hand shape can make it much easier to reach fourth finger in tune.

Scales are an obvious means of introducing finger patterns, but it is not enough for students to understand key signatures; they must also gain the coordination to execute the new patterns. Do plenty of drills, sliding fingers from their more common position to the lowered or extended locations. (Be sure to clarify any confusion between "normal" positions and "natural" notes.) Take time to teach fingerboard mapping. I feel that many intonation problems are due to a lack of awareness of half steps. Have students practice half-step and whole-step trills to refine technique and intonation. Chromatic scales are also excellent for exploring the fingerboard thoroughly and reinforcing half-step concepts. Use whatever method works for you, but drill, drill, drill finger patterns! Otherwise, students are likely to settle for a vague out-of-tune-ness between notes I call "shar-naturals" because they're neither sharp *nor* natural. I also call it Neverland because it doesn't exist in reality, and they should "never land in Neverland!"

Tone: Developing the Right Hand and Bow Control

Some methods of bow-hold instruction focus on showing students where to put their fingers, but I think it's important for them to experience how their hand should *feel* in relation to the bow. It is extremely important for them to learn to relax and use weight instead of tension in holding and moving the bow. I have students learn on pencils because they are light (thus avoiding unnecessary tension) and are readily available so they can practice throughout the day. ("Sure, you can practice your bow hold in math class!")

I introduce the following five steps:

1. Holding the end of a pencil with the left hand at arm's length in front of the body, **hang** the creases of the fingers of the right hand on top of the pencil. Take a moment to bounce up and down, feeling the weight of the hand and arm on the pencil. Bring the pencil toward the body without dropping the elbows.
2. **Roll** the hand (pronate) toward the index finger, as if turning a doorknob to the left or pouring a saltshaker. It is extremely important for the elbow to be level with the hand; otherwise, students are likely to supinate or have an awkward bend in the wrist. Violin and viola players will pronate more than cello and bass players.
3. Violin and viola players will **set the pinky** on top of the pencil so the finger is curved, pointing straight down. Tap up and down to test for control, alleviate tension, and reinforce the correct shape. Be sure the pinky is close enough to the ring finger that it can round. When transitioning from the pencil to the bow, I add a pinky cup cut from vinyl tubing to support the correct pinky shape. (Cello and bass players skip this step, as their pinkies will continue to lie flat against the frog.)
4. **Set the thumb** so the tip is pointing straight up at the pencil, positioned just behind the middle finger. The contact point should be the inside corner of the thumb next to the nail. All knuckles should remain rounded out so that they are relaxed and flexible. Most bow-hold problems are due to squeezing with the thumb, which is why I position it last.
5. **Almost let go** of the pencil with the right hand so there is no chance of squeezing. Many beginning students try so hard to

manage their position that they squeeze like crazy, resulting in tension in the hand and arm and the typical beginner's scratchy tone.

All beginners (as well as students that need remedial work) should repeat these steps until they become a habit. Correct bow-hold habits are more likely to result in ease of playing, clear tone, flexibility, and coordination.

Set-Up/Fundamentals: Instrument Position and Body Alignment

Violin and viola players should stand at first to avoid bad habits. Cellists should sit at the front edge of their seats; bass players will either stand or (preferably) use a stool that is appropriate for their height. Violins and violas need to be positioned on the left shoulder, level with the ground, and supported with the weight of the head so the left hand can function freely. Cello endpins should be extended until the scroll is level with the student's nose when the student is standing. When seated, cellists should position their feet on either side of the instrument, knees below the C bout, with the C peg near their left ear. Bassists should place the endpin in front of their left foot and lean the instrument toward them so that the back right edge contacts the belt area above the left leg. The nut of the bass fingerboard should be level with their eyebrow. Cello and bass fingerboards should be close to the left ear, as though the left hand (in first position) is holding a phone to the ear for bassists or chin for cellists. All students should have their elbows away from their bodies, a straight line from their elbow to the back of their hand, with no bend in the wrist. Violin and viola players should only contact the neck of the instrument at the base of the index finger and the tip of the thumb, so there is space in the thumb valley with the palm hanging straight down. All players should maintain an easy balance with freedom to sway slightly in any direction. Hips and shoulders should be in alignment, head balanced on top of a straight spine. It is easy for students to take these instructions lightly, as though they aren't important, but if they see pictures of ideal vs. less-than-ideal position, they can usually agree that you can't play like a pro if you look like a beginner. Without good basic technique, students will find it impossible to play fast, play in tune, do vibrato, or shift effectively.

Ensemble Playing: Unity, Precision, Tempo Stability

One of the most reliable methods I know for tightening ensemble playing is to have the group play pizzicato. That way they can hear exactly when to place notes which might otherwise sound muddy with bows. This is, of course, assuming that they all understand the rhythm, which may not be the case. Find out by having them clap and count rhythms. It may be helpful to have them clap and count or air-bow while you demonstrate the excerpt and then have them play while you clap/count.

Tempo stability is most often a problem of rushing. Students are either anxious about keeping up or lack the experience to feel the subdivision of the pulse. Have them play all subdivided note values (like eighth notes within quarter notes, or sixteenths within eighth notes) with separate bows while you (or part of the group) play the music as written, making sure the notes line up on the correct beats. Then switch and have them play as printed while you (or part of the group) subdivide.

Another excellent strategy for internalizing the pulse is to have students play what I call the Beat Subtraction Game. Start by having everyone clap a steady (repeating) four-quarter-note pattern, counting aloud. When you indicate, have them rest on one of the beats (for example, beat 1), bouncing their hands to the side on the rest. Continue the pattern with rests on beat 1, and call out another beat to rest on. Repeat until only one note remains, then have them only clap that beat every other measure. Have them stop counting aloud so that they have to count in their heads, then stop bouncing hands on the rests. The result is pure magic as they discover the group's ability to feel the pulse, and clap in unison, notes that are two measures apart.

Expression: Phrasing, Balance, Dynamic Contrast

There are many aspects that contribute to expressive playing, such as vibrato, bow distribution, and tone, but it is extremely important for students to incorporate breathing and movement in the early stages of playing. It would be very awkward to try to play expressively while sitting rigidly and holding one's breath, but you can't just say "Move!" Students need more specific direction. To begin with, I teach students to "lift and sniff" on the prep beat, just as a conductor would give a cue, in the style and speed of the upcoming music. (Violin and viola players lift their scrolls, cello and bass players nod their heads and, if appropriate, lift their bow arms.) The best imagery I've ever heard for connecting breath with movement is to imagine a sail on the bow just in front of the hand, and the player must blow on the sail to get it to move. If the player wants the bow to move slowly and gently, they will inhale and blow in a similar manner. If they want the bow to move more forcefully or with greater attack, the inhale and exhale will be sharp with fast air. We want students to feel freedom of motion, but at first the motion needs some choreography. Have violin and viola players stand with their weight on their right foot, cello and (seated) bass players sit with weight on their right sitz bone. As they perform a slow down-bow, they should rock their weight to the left. Performing an up-bow, their weight will shift from left to right. Violin and viola players may also slightly swing their instruments to the left on the down-bow and to the right on the up-bow.

In order to achieve a full range of expression, students should explore the spectrum of intensity in vibrato (fast/slow, wide/narrow), dynamics, articulation, and bow speed. Each of these techniques should be practiced individually for mastery and then applied to the music the students are working on. It can also be extremely helpful for them to watch or listen to advanced musicians to get a sense of style to emulate. If possible, demonstrate passages with and without expression so students get a sense of their musical options.

Articulation Control

Beginning students often learn the physicality of detaché and staccato using the Suzuki-based "Mississippi Hot Dog" rhythm, also known in my classroom as the "Oily, Oily Elbow" rhythm (four detaché eighth notes and two staccato quarter notes). Placing the bow slightly lower than the middle, the student will open and close the elbow—as though they've put an invisible drop of oil on a rusty hinge—in a loose, repetitive motion for the detaché notes and stop the bow for the staccato notes.

Martelé is the next bow stroke I teach. Just as students would do pizzicato by applying pressure to the string with their finger and letting it go, they apply pressure with the bow (diagonally downward) and suddenly release as they pull a down-bow or up-bow. **Martelé** is a ballistic motion, much like a bullet being shot from a gun; once the initial force is released, the bow drifts to a stop before being initiated in the other direction. In more simple terms: "Pop and go!"

Legato and spiccato both require sophisticated technique. Once a characteristic bow hold has been established, students need to develop flexibility so the hand can respond like a shock absorber to the friction of the bow against the string. The base knuckles need to be relatively flat, allowing the other knuckles to be round and flexible. In order to achieve smooth legato bow strokes, the fingers need to be passive and respond as the bow changes direction. Spiccato can be thought of as a detaché stroke with lifted edges. Just like with detaché, the elbow needs to open and close so the student doesn't swing from the shoulder. It is typically done at the balance point, and the tempo needs to be sufficiently fast for the motion to be repetitive, allowing the bow to bounce. If the student has not gained flexibility and control with their technique, their spiccato will likely be stiff and sound scratchy. For a brushy spiccato, keep the stroke fairly horizontal, only slightly lifting in a U-shape. For sharper articulation, allow the stroke to bounce more vertically, using less horizontal motion.

It is also important for students to understand the variety of sounds they can achieve with articulation. Demonstrate articulations verbally by slurring words, then enunciating them clearly. (For example, "habby birvday" vs. "happy birthday.") In music, articulation refers to the attack (or lack thereof) at the beginning of a note. Using a variety of bow techniques, we can achieve a spectrum of sounds, such as "wah," "lah," "mah," "bah," "pah," "kah," and "tah." Students can experiment with bow weight, speed, contact point, and placement (from frog to tip) to achieve a variety of articulations. Much like a painter utilizing a spectrum of shade and color, musicians use articulation to express musical ideas.

Repertoire
Repertoire is *extremely* important for the success of your program. If it is too easy, your students will be bored, but if it is too difficult, they will be frustrated and may give up. The music you choose must be challenging enough for students to be proud to play but attainable for their level. Even if you use a method book in conjunction with orchestra music, you will be teaching or reinforcing new techniques with the music, so consider what you want students to learn from the music. I like to program a variety of styles for each concert: at least one piece of classical music, one in a dramatic minor key, one beautiful slow piece, and one pop/show tune that they're sure to enjoy.

If you find you've chosen a piece that the students really dislike, it may be best to cut your losses and switch pieces. I recently chose a piece that half of the group loved and the other half hated; it was one of the most difficult semesters for group morale I've ever experienced! On the other hand, sometimes you can find that one piece that everyone loves and can't wait to play each day. I know I've done well when every time I call a tune someone in the room exclaims, "Yes, that's my favorite song!" Here are my (current) top ten pieces for middle school string players:

- "Dragonhunter," by Richard Meyer
- "Gauntlet," by Doug Spata
- "Jupiter" from *The Planets*, by Gustav Holst, arr. by Deborah Baker Monday
- "Tango Espressivo," by Matt Turner
- "Blue Rhythmico," by Kirt N. Mosier
- "Medieval Wars," by Brian Balmages
- "Pirates Legend," by Soon Hee Newbold
- "March of the Meistersingers," by Richard Wagner, arr. by Sandra Dackow
- "Libertango," by Astor Piazzolla, arr. by James Kazik
- "My Shot" from *Hamilton*, by Lin-Manuel Miranda, arr. by Larry Moore

Recruiting/Community Building

Performances, competitions and trips can be rewarding, but don't underestimate your own influence on a daily basis.

Recruitment of beginners takes place in the spring so that we can anticipate class size for the following fall. Elementary instrumental teachers go school to school as a group, performing band and orchestra music and demonstrating each of the instruments. Students are given information about the programs and sign-up forms to be returned. It can also be helpful to give potential students a chance to get hands-on experience with instruments they're interested in. Kids are much more likely to stick with an instrument if it is a good match for them. This can also be a great opportunity for older students to help out, acting as role models for the younger kids and showing pride in their program.

Once students have joined the music program, the challenge is to retain them over time. It is extremely important for them to feel successful and part of an "in" crowd. Performances, competitions, and trips can be rewarding, but don't underestimate your own influence on a daily basis. You, the teacher, create the environment in your class, so try to keep things positive as you insist on high standards. Choosing fun, challenging music the students are proud to play is also a very important element. If possible, let your classes play for each other or, even better, mentor younger groups. Each fall, my youth orchestra students host String Mentor Day and work side-by-side with recent beginners. It's immensely helpful for the beginners to get one-on-one help, and the older kids love sharing their expertise. At the end of the event, the youth orchestra performs for the beginners and their families so they can see where they may be in another year or two.

Margaret Selby

"Focus determines success."

Margaret Selby *is the orchestra director at Laing Middle School in Charleston, South Carolina, where she built the program from 42 to 215 students in 5 years. Mrs. Selby's orchestras regularly earn superior ratings at SCMEA Concert Performance Assessment and other festivals in the southeast. She has adjudicated orchestra festivals in South Carolina and Las Vegas and has been the guest conductor at numerous district and regional honors orchestras throughout the state of South Carolina. Mrs. Selby was the 2015–17 president of the South Carolina Music Educators Association Orchestra Division and is a registered Suzuki cello teacher. She was a co-presenter at the 2012 ASTA National Conference in Atlanta, Georgia, and has performed with the South Carolina Philharmonic and the Charleston Symphony. She earned her degrees in music education and performance from the University of South Carolina and currently lives in Mt. Pleasant, South Carolina with her husband and two children.*

Rehearsal Philosophy

I aim to have specific, stepwise, and accomplishable goals for students to achieve and feel successful during each rehearsal. I make music rehearsals fun, but I also want students to learn how hard work leads to success. I want students to learn self-awareness that will help them improve not only their own playing but also how they relate to their section so that they can become a meaningful contributor to the entire ensemble. Sometimes teaching music is secondary to teaching students how to be independent thinkers, and the quote displayed in my classroom is "Focus Determines Success."

Rehearsal Preparation
Long- and Short-Range Planning
I have clear expectations and goals for what students are to accomplish in their middle school orchestra experience and what they need to learn to be prepared for high school orchestra. I have long- and short-range goals for right-hand skills, left-hand skills, key studies (scales, arpeggios, etc.), music literacy, and ensemble skills. I break down the large goals into semester or quarterly goals, and then I make weekly goals and daily plans to accomplish those goals. I refer to my long-term goals often to stay on track and to avoid getting bogged down.

Each middle school program is different, and in each of my teaching situations, I consider what can be accomplished within the realities of the situation. For example, teachers who only see students every other day for 40 minutes must plan for what can be done in that amount of time. In general, I divide class time into two or three parts: 20–30 percent warm-up, 20–30 percent new skills, 40–50 percent ensemble skills/concert music rehearsal. The percentage of time for activities is adjusted according to what is needed in each part of the school year. More time is devoted to the warm-up and new skills at the beginning of the year or semester verses more time on ensemble skills and concert music closer to performances.

Class Preparation
Be prepared. Know what you want to accomplish, and have a plan. Have a routine, but mix it up every now and then. Try to predict what will challenge students or what they will need to know to be successful individually and as an ensemble. Play each part if you can. As a cellist, I try to play the upper string and bass parts before instructing the students. This helps me understand the students' perspectives, and I usually find challenges that I wouldn't have by just looking at the score. Break down the skills needed, and have as many strategies to improve them as you can. What works with one group may not work for another.

Teach procedures for as many classroom or rehearsal routines as possible. Establish how the students enter the room, set up, unpack, and begin class. Also, include how they ask to go to the bathroom, leave their seat, pass out new music, make activity transitions, and end and leave class. This will foster a smooth class experience, and you will have more time and energy to work toward making music.

Classroom Management
I have students set a timer at the beginning of each class. They must work together to go through their beginning-of-class procedures (set up, unpack, and tune individually and as an ensemble). If they can do the whole routine in less time than assigned, they can bank the extra time in the Time Bank posted on the board. Once they have earned an amount of time equivalent to an entire class period, they get to cash in for a rewards day where they choose their musically related activity for a day. Activities may include: Music Game Day (Musical Chairs using recordings of our current concert music, Musical Bingo, Musical Twister, etc.), YouTube Day (string-related videos), Movie Music Day, Instrument Switch Day (the students teach each other a secondary instrument), Electric Instrument/Alternative Instrument Day, etc.

The Time Bank has been highly effective at creating an efficient start to class. Even some of the least motivated classes will work hard to earn a rewards day. It also helps during the entire class period because while time can be earned, it can also be taken away if the group wastes rehearsal time. My beginners usually start with seven minutes as the goal set-up time after much practicing to master the routine. Each time they earn a rewards day, the expectation is raised and they have less allowed time. By the time they are in the second or third year, they can accomplish all of the starting routine in under three minutes. It must be mentioned that we tune by ear and then check the tuning with electronic tuners. Because this is a student-led activity, I am able to use this time to record attendance, repair instruments, help students with pegs, etc.

I also use as much non-verbal communication as possible. Hand signals are great!

Warm-Up

The warm-up is where we review fundamentals and learn new technique. I believe that review is where the best learning happens because we can go deeper into a concept. It is important to do daily review of instrument placement, bow-hand and left-hand position, tone/bow usage, intonation/ finger patterns, and scales/arpeggios. Each skill is reviewed and can be further refined daily. New skills can then be built upon the established skills. I try to do a routine that reviews all of these skills daily or at least a rotation that reviews all of the skills over the course of the week. Much of it can be done nonverbally with teacher or student leaders modeling for the class.

At least once per week, we start our warm-up with string calisthenics while listening to pop music. Who wouldn't want to start the day to "Eye of the Tiger" or "Another One Bites the Dust"? This is an energizing way to review sitting or standing position, instrument placement, and left-/ right-hand positions and motion. We do finger taps, bow pushups, shifting, vibrato motion, etc., all while grooving to the music. Sometimes I choose a song that is in an approachable key and the students do ear-training and improvising exercises as well. Students use listening skills to match the key center, melody, and accompaniment parts. Even at the beginner level, students can match notes and play rhythms that allow them to jam to the music. They love it! Just google "pop tunes in the key of (your choice)" or go to http://www.songkeyfinder.com.

I use many of the exercises in *Habits of a Successful Middle Level String Musician* for our warm-ups. For bow technique, we use the Open String Exercises and Bowing Variations. This is followed by a finger pattern exercise called the Tetrachord Etude and/or other left-hand exercises that include extensions, shifting, or vibrato. We play familiar scales and arpeggios to review skills before focusing on a new scale or other new skills (note-reading, rhythm, sight-reading, etc.).

Intonation and Fluency: Developing the Left Hand

Good intonation is the golden ticket for any orchestra. Everyone wants to play in tune, so why don't we? It takes great discipline, persistence, and awareness. It's not easy, but it is absolutely possible, even for a beginner class. We have to expect our students to play in tune from the very beginning. This can be tedious work, and it is easy for a teacher to get complacent and allow students to play out of tune. I have to constantly stop and ask myself questions like "Are they really in tune?" "Are the half steps close enough?" "Do they sound like the New York Philharmonic yet?" If not, there is more to do. Recording the class performance is a valuable tool for teachers and students alike.

I teach students what good intonation sounds like. I also teach them what a pitch sounds like when it is too high or too low and how to adjust it. They love playing intonation games. Favorite games include:

- **Find the Rosin (or other object).** The "seeker" students close their eyes while the teacher hides the rosin with the rest of the class watching. Then the seeker tries to find the rosin by using clues given to them by the sounds of the class. The class plays a designated note too high or low according to how close the student is to the hidden rosin. The closer the student is to the rosin, the more in tune they play, and vice versa. This can also be used to teach dynamics as well (louder is closer; softer is farther away).
- **Where's Waldo? Everyone closes their eyes while the teacher taps one or more students on the shoulder to indicate who is to play a note too high or too low.** Then the student who is "it" has to find the out-of-tune note (and correct them if possible).

Teaching finger patterns and fingerboard mapping is essential. My favorite and most effective intonation tool is the Tetrachord Etude from *Habits of a Successful Middle Level String Musician.* The beginners learn about whole and half steps. They memorize the Dorian tetrachord version first (E, F♯, G, A) and work hard to play it perfectly in tune by singing, matching/adjusting pitch, and playing with a drone. When we achieve our goal, we move to other finger patterns and do the same work until each finger pattern is in tune. This can also be applied to correcting intonation in concert music. There is often a passage where the intonation issue can be solved by clarifying the finger patterns and simply stopping to play the corresponding tetrachord etude or any tune that they know well by ear that also uses the same finger pattern.

Cello Left-Hand Position

The cello left-hand thumb is extremely important. As I tell my students, "C is for cello." The thumb should be curved under the second finger and lightly touching under the D string on the back of the neck. The elbow or "wing" needs to be high enough to support the hand as it moves to each string, so it should be higher while playing on the lower strings but not too low on the upper strings. To help students remember the height of the elbow (this also works for the upper strings' left wrist), I always say "Don't be an overachiever or underachiever; be average." The left-hand knuckles should be curved or "curly" and react like shock absorbers while the weight being put on the string is coming from the arm, not the thumb. The wrist is flat, and, using their "sly fox eyes" or a sideways glance, a student should be able to see all the way down the arm from the curved finger knuckles. Do not allow students to turn their head to look at their left hand because it usually alters their entire position and creates problems. Try holding a piece of paper between a student's head and cello neck or have them look at different spots around the room while they play to prevent them from watching their hand.

Extensions

When teaching extensions, I teach backward extensions first because only the first finger moves and the remainder of the hand frame is maintained. I remind the students that it is okay to touch the string more on the side of the fingertip of the first finger. It won't be the same feeling as their original position. The back of the hand's angle and the elbow stay the same while the first finger steps backward.

For forward extensions, remind the students that the extension takes place between the first and second finger and is a whole step. The thumb steps or slides forward to move with the second finger. This is probably the most important step that I remind students to check daily. Like backward extensions, the first finger will probably touch the string on more of the side of the fingertip. Make sure the students keep the first finger on the string and maintain their left-hand frame while they move the thumb and the second, third, and fourth fingers forward. Avoid twisting or turning the back of the hand toward the floor. The elbow should be supporting the motion. They should be able to "see their invisible watch," or I've even seen a teacher balance a coin on the back of a student's hand while doing extensions.

Tone: Developing the Right Hand and Bow Control

Tone

The bow makes the sound. That sounds so obvious, but as string players, students forget because they are so focused on the left-hand skills. Beginner band classes talk about making a characteristic tone frequently. Many band directors cannot make a perfect tone on all of the instruments they teach, but they bring in guest instructors or play recordings of great players for the students to get a clear idea of the sound they are trying to produce. We need to make sure our students have great models for tone. Most of the time, our students do not come to class with a clear idea of a beautiful string tone, and we are their only source. Model for your students as much as possible, or have them listen to recordings of great tone.

Bow-Hand Position

Great tone cannot be created without a relaxed and flexible bow hand position. I teach the initial hand placement on a pencil and a drinking straw before moving to the bow. We spend a lot of time perfecting each step before earning our "License to Bow." After making the transition to the bow and starting to make sound, I find that one of the most important keys to success for keeping relaxed bow hands is for the students to rest the bow on the string before moving the hand to it. While the bow is resting, they need to check that their thumb and pinky fingers (pinky tap) are curved and relaxed. Setting the bow before playing will also help the class play together as an ensemble later.

I create position checklists and mantras that we use every time we put the bow on the string during at least the first six months. My students and I chant, "Curve your thumb, don't be glum. Curve your pinky, don't be stinky" (from Lenny Schranze at the University of Memphis), or "Roll the Bow (Stick) Toward the Scroll" for correct angle and bow-arm height. I like to use a count-off, such as "Set the bow, pinky tap, curve the thumb, ready-breathe (go)!" or "Curve all fingers, pour the bow (put the weight toward the first finger), tap the pinky, ready-go!" (Selby). My students also love to perform bow songs like "Up Like a Rocket" (from the Suzuki Method) or "The Wheels on the Bus." The more games and songs we use, the better. Flexibility and movement are the key. Keep checking bow holds for improvement, especially as the students grow so fast in middle school. I try to make every day bow hand day!

Bow Speed, Bow Lanes, and Weight

Middle school students can improve their tone quickly and easily by learning the three factors of tone production. Early on, we start talking about bow lanes (contact point), bow speed, and weight. I draw a diagram on the board of the bow lanes, with Lane 5 being closest to the bridge, Lane 3 directly between the bridge and fingerboard, and Lane 1 over the bottom edge of the fingerboard. Some teachers may have the numbers in the opposite order, but use whatever works for you. We then experiment with the three factors of tone production in each bow lane and make all kinds of horror movie sounds (which we use in our October concert when we make a ghost story). Our goal is to make a good tone in each bow lane. Students quickly learn that they must use a heavier, slow bow while playing in Lane 5 near the bridge and use a lighter, faster bow in Lane 1 or 2 near the fingerboard. Sometimes it is also fun to do the "white stripe" contest to see if they are truly staying in the designated bow lane. Have the students wipe off all rosin from the strings. Then, have them put fresh rosin on the bow. Tell them which bow lane is assigned, and have them play a scale or passage from their music. The rosin will make a white stripe or mark that will tell them and you if they stayed in their lane.

When adjudicating orchestras, one of the most common comments that I give for tone improvement is for students to work on using a faster bow with their contact point closer to the bridge. Talking about bow speed also helps with bow distribution and note duration.

A common game for changing bow speed begins with students playing an open string or scale with a metronome. The teacher writes numbers on the board, like a fake phone number or any random set of numbers. The students have to a use a whole bow and count the number of beats for each of the numbers written on the board. For example, if the teacher wrote "4, 3, 2, 1, 2, 3, 4" on the board, the students would play a whole bow with four beats for the first down-bow, a faster whole bow using three beats for the up-bow, an even faster down-bow with two beats on the next bow, and so on.

Set-Up/Fundamentals: Instrument Position and Body Alignment

Insist that students have great posture and position at all times. The Suzuki Method says that it takes 10,000 repetitions before a motion or skill feels

112

natural. Of course, whatever we do repeatedly will begin to feel "right" so it is important that our students practice good posture and movement correctly. Middle school is awkward! Keep checking their ever-changing positions as the students grow and change. I often ask students to check their neighbor. Sometimes they can more easily see their neighbor's position, and it's amazing how quickly they will correct their own in response.

Golden Nuggets for Cello Position

Many students and teachers struggle to find the correct endpin height/angle for their cellists of all body types. I learned this trick from Suzuki Method teachers: Have the student sit on the edge of the chair with their feet flat on the floor in front of the chair's front legs. The body should be balanced and leaning slightly forward with the hands on their knees. The teacher places the cello on the student's body without using the endpin. The teacher uses the checklist below to make sure the cello is properly placed on the student's body before lengthening the endpin to rest on the floor and naturally hold the cello where it already rests on the student. The student should be able to hug the cello comfortably, and the cello should not be pushing them back.

1. *Feet:* Flat on the floor.
2. *Knees:* The bottom C bout points should be at or above the knees.
3. *Heart:* Cello resting comfortably on the chest.
4. *Neck Near the Neck:* Keep the cello neck near the student's neck. Some students will try to look at their left hand, and the cello will start to drift to the side. This will cause major left-hand/arm problems. We use "sly fox eyes" (sideways glances) to look at our left hand if needed.
5. *Ear Tickle:* Shaking the head "no" should allow the C peg to gently touch the ear. This helps to keep students from having the scroll/cello too high.

My students use the bold words above to quickly check and review their position during each class.

Ensemble Playing: Unity, Precision, Tempo Stability

I have these seven goals for ensemble skills (courtesy of Christopher Selby) posted on my classroom wall:

- Breathe, move, cue, and perform together in synchrony with other musicians.
- Perform accurate rhythms together within a synchronized pulse and a musically convincing tempo.
- Use the same bow weight, speed, and contact point as the other members of the section to create a well-blended ensemble tone and timbre.
- Finely tune one's own notes to be in tune with other musicians.
- Perform the same bowings, articulations, and styles in the same part of the bow as other members of one's section.
- Use a volume that blends with the section, that balances the importance of one's own part with respect to the parts of other sections of the ensemble, and that agrees with other players through the peaks, valleys, and points in between of all dynamics and phrasing.
- Convey clear and musically expressive ideas that go beyond the notes on the page; these musical concepts include character, style, interpretation, beauty, intensity, mood, and emotion.

My goal is to teach students to become self-aware and to ask themselves if they are doing each of these actions. I strive to teach them to listen, watch, and match/blend with their section and other parts the orchestra. We practice breathing and moving together.

It is very important that students practice performing outside the classroom "bubble." They need to learn to adjust to different acoustics as an ensemble. I once took a very fine sixth-grade group to a festival. They sounded amazing in the warm-up room and then panicked on stage because the acoustics were so contrasting. I learned a valuable lesson. They had not had a chance to perform outside of the classroom, so they were only used to one type of sound. From that day forward, I started asking students to pick up their music stands and follows me for "field trips" all over the school. We play outside, in the cafeteria, in the front office (this can be a win-win with your administration), etc. For the times that we can't leave the classroom or we don't have enough time to do anything drastic, I simply move to the other side of the room and have them turn their chairs to face me. If nothing else, it gets them out of their comfort zones. The concert will never feel like a comfort zone, so I try to get them used to feeling a bit uncomfortable.

One of my favorite ensemble and listening activities is "scattered seating." Once the students have a solid grasp of their concert pieces, at least once per week, we have a day where they must change seats in the orchestra. This also works well in an honors orchestra setting. They cannot sit with their stand partner and must sit next to someone who plays a different part. We try to have all of the parts evenly spread across the room, and yes, I always laugh when the basses come right up front. It's amazing how changing seats can change the sound. The students (and teacher) usually hear parts they may not have heard before. This also forces students to be more independent. Problems with balance, dynamics, and rhythmic precision are usually exposed and improved with this exercise.

Expression: Phrasing, Balance, Dynamic Contrast
Middle school students may be dramatic in the hallway while talking to their friends, but they are usually much more reserved when it comes to making music. They may believe they are making a crescendo when only a faint change in volume is actually heard. Students are very capable of making beautifully contrasting dynamics and phrasing if they plan exactly how they will use their bow. What part of the bow, how much bow speed and weight, and what bow lane or contact point is needed? We experiment with how to create the sound we want using the previous questions and then write many detailed instructions in the concert music, including key words like: bridge, frog, fast bow, tip, save bow, vibrate, set bow, etc. We frequently record our class performance and listen to determine if what we are trying to express (or what is written in the music) is coming across to the audience. Exaggeration is a must. For example, start crescendos softer to create larger crescendos. Singing is also a great tool when students are not sure what to do with a phrase.

Articulation Control
Be specific about the part of the bow to be used, the contact point (bow lane), and amount of bow speed needed to produce the correct sound. It's always a good idea to check the bow hand's flexibility, too. Modeling is usually most effective for students. Students must listen and adjust their sound to match the group.

Repertoire
Repertoire selection is one of the most important things we plan for each year. I spend hours and sometimes days trying to find the right piece for a

particular group. I believe that the correct piece should be the application of skills that a group already has. It should not apply skills that are at the cutting edge of the students' ability but slightly below. This allows the group to focus on ensemble skills and creating a polished performance. I try to pick a variety of works and sometimes we have themed concerts. Some of my favorite middle school pieces include:

- "String Explosion," by Frank Rodgers
- "Russian Music Box," by Soon Hee Newbold
- "Burst," by Brian Balmages
- "Fantasia on a Japanese Folk Song," by Brian Balmages
- "Dragon Hunter," "Kabuki Dance," and "Night Shift," by Richard Meyer (really, everything by him)
- "Accents," by Robert Frost
- "Red Pepper and Orange Jam," by Jeffrey Bishop
- "Ukrainian Bell Carol," by John Caponegro
- "Fantasia on an Original Theme," by Joseph Phillips
- "Red Lodge Reel," by Bob Phillips
- "M to the Third Power," by Carold Nunez
- "Bashana Haba'Ah," by Hirsch/arr. Conley
- "Country Wedding" from *The Moldau*, by Smetana/arr. Dackow

Recruiting/Community Building
It starts by creating a class where students feel successful every day.

I try to show my passion for music and teaching every day. I try to be a person who people want to be around. It starts by creating a class where students feel successful every day. Have fun! If we're not having fun in my class, I know something isn't working.

It's time to go recruiting. What do I do?

- **Communicate through multiple outlets.** Use email, brochures, school newsletters, signs, demos, social media, the school website, whatever it takes!
- **Create a flyer/brochure with information about your program.** I include answers to FAQs about scheduling, instrument rentals, etc. I list the fun activities we will be doing, including concerts and our field trip to perform at a theme park.

- **Create quality live or video presentations.** You are a sales-person for your program, so be exciting and energetic. If you perform or have a group perform, make sure it sounds and looks great. Play music the perspective students will like and want to learn. We always play current movie or pop tunes.
- **Help at the feeder schools' programs.** I always help tune at the fifth-grade concerts.
- **Talk to the prospective students in large and small groups.** Either can be effective, but when possible, I schedule 10-minute classroom visits with every fifth grade class. Talking to a smaller group gives me a chance to make a more personal connection with the potential students. With 10-minute visits, I talk about what we offer and all the fun music and activities we will be doing. With a larger group presentation and more time, I briefly demonstrate each instrument as well.
- **Recruit beginners *and* continuing students.** In my school district, the strings program begins in fifth grade, but I encourage any sixth grader to join the orchestra even if they have no experience. This creates a class with students at different levels, but I find that by the end of the first semester, most of the students are at nearly the same level. When possible, don't exclude any student who wants to play.
- **Make it easy to sign up.** I have a brochure with a sign-up form on it that I have available at all events where potential students are present. I give out hard copies to every student during class visits, fifth grade concerts, and school tours. I also send electronic copies to all rising sixth graders through the fifth-grade teachers (be sure to have a good relationship with those teachers!) and post it on the school website. I encourage parents to return it by whatever means is the easiest for them (email, fax, mail, in person, etc.). My sign-up form is in addition to the school's class selection process, but having a separate form allows me to create a potential list of students that I can use in advance of the approaching school year to give to the person in charge of scheduling to help catch mistakes, and it also provides me with more concrete numbers of students, which can help with my requests for more class sections/scheduling, equipment/supplies, staffing, and general planning for the year.
- **Create good PR.** Have group t-shirts and/or other gear. We plan to wear them every Friday and for certain concerts.

Mimi Zweig

> "Violin performance engages the physical,
> the psychological, and the musical abilities
> of the player. Learning is based on natural
> physical motions nurtured in a nonjudgmental
> environment."

Mimi Zweig *is currently Professor of Violin at the Jacobs School of Music and Director of the Indiana University String Academy. She is in her fourth decade of teaching at Indiana University. Since 1972, she has developed pre-college string programs across the United States and has presented master classes and pedagogy workshops in the United States, Mexico, Canada, Israel, Japan, Argentina, Brazil, and Europe. She produced Mimi Zweig StringPedagogy.com, an innovative web-based teaching tool. In the spring of 2006, American Public Television released the Emmy-nominated documentary,* Circling Around: The Violin Virtuosi, *featuring String Academy students. Her students have won numerous competitions and teach and perform worldwide.*

Rehearsal Philosophy

My basic philosophy regarding rehearsing is to break problems down to the lowest common denominator. It is then possible to fix problems one at a time, knowing that all mistakes occur between two notes. By the end of every rehearsal, progress is accomplished in intonation, ensemble, articulation, and musical phrasing. Students become excited as they hear this process unfold, which spurs them on to more practicing.

Rehearsal Preparation

I create a detailed plan of how I will approach each new piece of music. Fingerings, bowings, isolating the difficulties, and understanding the form/ structure of the music are first on the list. After the initial rehearsal, I hand the students the responsibility of learning their parts individually.

Warm-Up

Warming up is accomplished by playing fast passages slowly, playing resonant tones using scales and open strings, reviewing shifting principles, and reminding students of the basic physical set-up.

Intonation and Fluency: Developing the Left Hand

Intonation and fluency are more easily developed if the student has a physically natural and relaxed set-up of the left and right hands. If there is excessive tension in the hands, the neck, the back, or even the toes, it is more difficult to play sensitively, in tune, and fast. Understanding the code of whole steps and half steps on individual strings and across the strings gives a clear picture of the geography of the fingerboard. Shifting is a topic unto itself. Many students are "jumpers," not understanding that there is an art to getting from one note to the next. Shifting takes many years to develop, but it begins with slow and light shifts timed with the pulse. Silent shifts are coordinated to occur on the old beat, arriving on the new note, on the new beat, and shifting with the old finger. In a bow change, this means that shifting occurs on the old bow and arriving on the new note and new bow simultaneously. Expressive shifts (which are incorporated later in a student's development) are timed to take place on the new beat with the new finger with infinite possibilities of speed and finger pressure.

Tone: Developing the Right Hand and Bow Control

Right-hand technique is based on flowing physical motions. I use the phrase, "No hold, bow hold" consistently. This gives students the sensation of not squeezing the bow. The thumb tends to be the biggest culprit in the bow "grip" because it likes to press up from under the stick. Actually,

119

the thumb should rest and balance on the side of the stick facing us. This enables us to have the feeling of pushing and pulling the string, releasing the resonance. To find the most beautiful tone, understanding the forces is crucial. The upward force of the violin counterbalances the downward weight of the bow arm, producing a tone without tension or squeezing.

Set-Up/Fundamentals: Instrument Position and Body Alignment

Awareness of our body tends to become a secondary concern as we learn how to play. However, in actuality, the body is the most important element in setting the balance of the instrument and bow. The relationship between the head, neck, and back stays flexible, allowing the body to lengthen. The head is connected to the neck and should not come forward; the chin does not want to find itself on the other side of the chin rest for violinists and violists. The jaw rests comfortably on the chin rest (I call it the jaw rest), and the fingerboard and bow can be viewed from the left eye.

One of the most important things I can say about the violin and body is to please not use a stiff shoulder rest when teaching children. Children are born with small necks, and only as they go into their teens do some necks grow longer. I use a thin sponge or dish shelving material to keep the violin from slipping and have recently found success using a shoulder pad developed by Eva Bogerin. If the violin is squeezed only with the head and the shoulder (with or without shoulder rest support), a tremendous amount of tension builds up in the neck and upper back muscles over the years. This leads to pains in the neck and shoulder and down the arms to the fingers. This tension limits the ability to be naturally musical, produce a beautiful tone, play in tune, and shift smoothly.

It is a misconception to think that the left hand/arm needs to be completely free of upper string instrument support duties. Ideally, the violin is balanced with interacting support from the head, collar bone, and left arm. From first to fifth position, this can be done by balancing the neck of the violin on the first finger's lowest knuckle and thumb. Above sixth position, the thumb can act as a hook holding up the neck. In conjunction with the pressure of a finger on the string, this allows movement of the violin up and down and side to side, freeing the shoulders and back. Students are convinced that their violins will fall to the ground without the head/shoulder support, but this is not possible if we think of the forces at work. We have an upward force from raising and lowering the violin with the left arm and the downward force of the weight of the right arm and bow. We can also think of supporting the violin by resting it gently against the body's neck, just as we can rest our bodies against a wall for unlimited support. The violin needs to be stable, but it is helpful to be able to move it slightly up and down and to the left and right for tone production and left-hand fluidity.

Ensemble Playing: Unity, Precision, Tempo Stability

I develop ensemble playing from the first beginning group classes. The five- and six-year-olds learn how to play together, lead together, and play in tune. As the students develop, the group repertoire becomes more complex, but the issues of ensemble, intonation, and tone are the same. In the more advanced group classes, music in two, three, and four parts is introduced into the repertoire. This training culminates in playing chamber music (mainly string quartets), in a chamber orchestra and in a large ensemble. It all works because the skills of playing together in an artistic way are all in place. Students that are set up in a natural way will have the ability to understand stability of tempo and nuances of phrasing.

Expression: Phrasing, Balance, Dynamic Contrast, Articulation Control

Phrasing, balance, dynamic contrast, articulation, and all the bow strokes develop when a student is well set up. Awareness of set-up begins with the first lessons and continues for a lifetime. A good foundation is laid with developing a balanced diet of repertoire, scales, and etudes.

Articulation Control

My bow stroke of choice is the **martelé**. It teaches the relationship between the string and hair when a resonant tone is produced. From the **martelé** stroke, the **detaché** and legato strokes are developed. The spiccato stroke is a **detaché** that comes slightly off the string and is played using the forearm in the lower half of the bow. The up- and down-bow staccato is an affirmation of the relationship of the hair to the string, with the string being pushed to the left on the up-bow and pulled to the right on the down-bow. When the toolbox of bow strokes, shifting, and vibrato are all in place, the musicality of the individual is released. No tools, no music.

Repertoire

"What is your favorite repertoire?" is a difficult question because I have students at every level, from the beginner to the artist level. My favorite pieces of all are the pieces that are played beautifully. I try to balance the journey of the students with repertoire, scales, and etudes. My repertoire list correlates repertoire with etudes. I am a firm believer in *Kreutzer Etudes* and often say I would not be able to teach the violin if Kreutzer had not lived. I will hear all of these etudes over the course of a student's study (after they have mastered *Wohlfhart Etudes*, op. 45, *Preparing for Kreutzer* by Harvey Whistler, *Trott Melodious Double Stops*, and *Schradieck School of Violin Technique*). It is important to have a good sequence of repertoire. (See Repertoire List: https://music.indiana.edu/precollege/year-round/strings/repertoire.shtml#rep)

Recruiting/Community Building

The best recruiting comes from the credibility of the product.

I have been the director of the Jacobs School of Music String Academy since 1976, when we began with six students. It quickly expanded to forty-five violin students, at which time a graduate assistant Rebecca Henry, currently co-chair of the Preparatory String Department at Peabody, joined the burgeoning String Academy. We currently have 160 students studying the violin, viola, and cello, and we have 12 teachers. The cello program, which has produced many young artist cellists, is directed by Susan Moses. My team of violin teachers includes Brenda Brenner. The best recruiting comes from the credibility of the product. If students are playing well and are happy, word gets around. Parents are always looking for excellence in the education of their children, and playing strings offers this challenge. Whether children and young adults decide to become professionals or not, they will always take with them the love of music and the fascination of studying a discipline in depth.

Appendix A.
Selected Repertoire

Analysis of Panel Favorites

Most Cited Favorite Pieces by Panel (Grades 1–4)

GRADE 1
"Canyon Sunset," by John Caponegro
"Dragonhunter," by Richard Meyer
"Fiddling A-Round," by John Caponegro

GRADE 2
"Gauntlet," by Doug Spata
"Night Shift," by Richard Meyer
"El Toro," by Don Brubaker

GRADE 3
"Lullaby," by William Hofeldt
"M to the Third Power," by Carold Nunez
"Somewhere" from *West Side Story*, by Leonard Bernstein/Moss

GRADE 4
"Allegro in D," by Antonio Vivaldi/Frackenpohl
"Hungarian Dance No. 5," by Johannes Brahms/Isaac
"Russian Sailor's Dance," by Rheinhold Gliere/Hoffman

Most Cited Favorite Composers (alphabetical order)
Brian Balmages
John Caponegro
Richard Meyer
Carold Nunez
Soon Hee Newbold
Bob Phillips
Doug Spata

Most Cited Favorite Arrangers (alphabetical order)
Sandra Dackow
Merle J. Isaac
Deborah Baker Monday

Repertoire Programming Philosophy
Sample Music Selection Criteria

I. Musical and Artistic Merit
- Expressive
- Enjoyable for performers, conductor, and audience

II. Educational Value and Playability
- Offers teaching potential
  - Reinforces concepts or skills currently being taught or previously taught
  - Motivating, student-friendly/age-appropriate techniques with some challenge
- Lies well on instruments
  - Avoids unnecessary awkward shifts, fingerings, and bowings
  - Appropriate key signatures, time signatures, rhythms for grade level
- Well-crafted/orchestrated
  - Melody shared by many instruments
  - Develops all/almost most players (not excessive rests or whole notes for some players)
  - Consistent challenge level (grade 2 piece does not spike up to grade 4 that can't be played well)
- Fits specific programming needs
  - Function (meets guidelines of festival, adjudication, or event)
  - Event (appropriately fits the context, location, and audience)
  - Strengths or weaknesses of the ensemble addressed or highlighted
  - Combination of piece with others on the program provide for solid opening, closing and variety

III. Balance and Variety
- Exposes students to a variety of styles, composers, and historical periods
- Balances traditional masterworks and great composers with newly composed music and students needs/interests
- Offers a variety of skills, bowings, techniques, tempos, and keys within the program and across the year(s) of playing
- Represents the music of a variety of cultural traditions

Appendix B.
Left Hand

Left-Hand Fingering Charts to Promote Accurate Visualization and Spacing of Fingers

These are often referred to as "finger patterns" by many of the panelists when discussing half- and whole-step placements.

Violin and Viola Fingering Chart

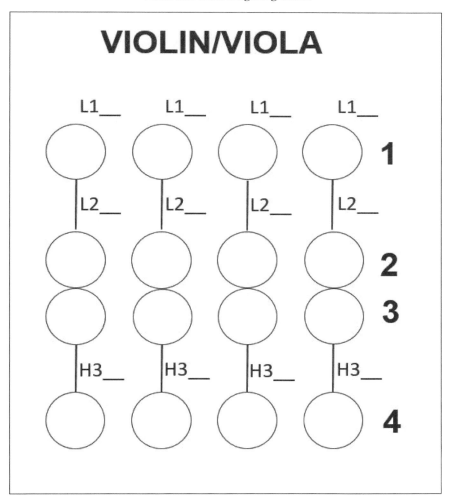

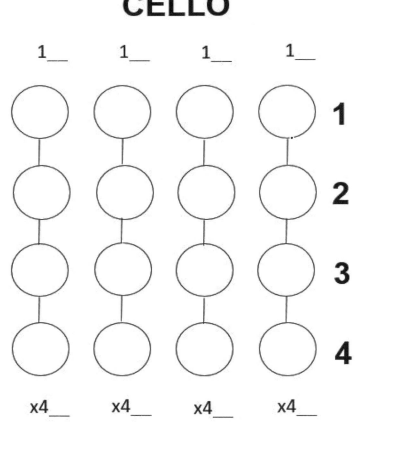

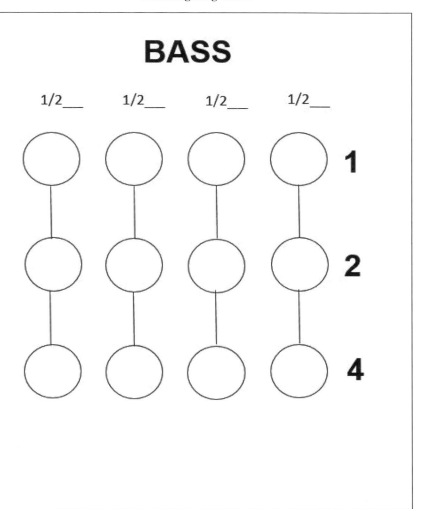

Appendix C.
Bow Hold and Bowing

Five Bow-Hold Set-Up Steps:
Teach students to remember "SPPPI: Shadow, Puppet, Place Pinky, Index." Chant these words every time students touch the bow during first weeks, and place them in count-offs as well.

1. *Shadow-dog:* Bow is held with two hands first and then in the air. Your thumb should be placed on the first line of your middle and ring fingers. Your thumb should be curved so that you create a circle shape with your hand.
2. *Puppet wrist:* Bend your right wrist up and down while maintaining the shadow-dog to relieve tension.
3. *Place*: Place the shadow-dog on the middle of the bow at the balance point. *Make sure that you are still holding the bow with two hands*. Maintain the circle shape established in the shadow-dog step. The bow should be placed at the first crease or line of your finger (violin/viola) or between your first and second crease (cello/bass).
4. *Pinky*: Curl your pinky and place it on top of the stick so that your fingernail touches wood (for violin and viola) or hangs over (cello or bass).
5. *Index*: Hang your index finger over the bow. Your hand should maintain the circular shape. Only now can you let go with your left hand.

Four Bow-Hold Checkpoints:
Teach students to remember "PATH: Pinky, Angle, Thumb, Hanging brothers."

- Pinky: Pinky should be curved and on top of the brown wood (fingernail can click the wood) for violins. Hanging over the stick for cello/bass.
- Angle: Fingers should be perpendicular to the stick (no tilt forward or back) for cello/bass, tilted left violin/viola.
- Thumb: The thumb should be curved and on the brown spot between the grip and frog—not poking through.

- Hanging Brothers: Middle fingers are hanging over the bow stick—not surfing on top.

Note: Fingers should be spread apart in a rounded (circular shape), not clumped tightly together in straight line.

License to Bow: Getting a Bowing Badge:

To get a license to bow (picture on page 72), require each student to demonstrate the five set-up steps and the four bow-hold checkpoints above, being sure that their hand looks like the picture on page 73. Students should be able to accurately place each finger on a pencil or a straw (without bending it with tension or squeezing) before they are allowed to bow on the string. Promote teamwork by encouraging everyone in the class to have a badge before the class can have "bow day." You might mark the significant class achievement by inviting the school resource officer to bestow licenses or play "Pomp and Circumstance" while the class processes in a bow-hold parade.

Bowing Instructional Sequence:

1. Perform bow-hold motions and exercises in the air (away from instruments).
2. Perform bow-hold motions on pencils (with flexibility exercises), "driving" their pencils on "highway" cards on their instrument.
3. Perform bow-hold motions on a straw (without bending it).
4. Test students until everyone earns a Bowing Badge!
5. Bow Day! Students make beginner bow holds at the balance point of the bow. They practice driving the bow straight on index cards with highway lines drawn on them (threaded through the strings of the instrument) before having cards individually removed at mastery. This allows them to visualize placement and correct motion.
6. Beginner bow-hold playing on all open string exercises and tunes they have already played.
7. Beginner bow-hold playing on all fingered tunes they have already played.
8. Advanced bow-hold (held at the frog) playing on all open string exercises and tunes they have already played.
9. Advanced bow-hold playing on all fingered tunes they have already played.

10. Advanced bow-hold playing on fingered notes while reading notation

Note: It is important not to add this sequence of skills before students have mastered appropriate instrument-holding position, sitting posture, and left-hand technique. Otherwise, students will likely sacrifice their technique in these areas to add new skills.

Appendix D.
Panel References and Resources to Explore

Rehearsal Preparation
"Fast and Efficient Ways to Prepare a Score" by Michael Alexander (2011). https://www.tmea.org/resources/southwestern-musician/archive/article?swm_id=161

Warm-Ups
"Daily Warm-up for Strings" by Michael Allen (1993). Hal Leonard Corporation.

"Expressive Techniques for Orchestra" by Kathleen DeBerry Brungard, Michael Alexander, Gerald Anderson, and Sandra Dackow (2011). Tempo Press.

"Habits of a Successful Middle-Level String Musician" by Christopher Selby and Scott Rush. GIA Publications.

"Rhythmic Projections: Rhythm Exercises for Building Mastery" by Seth Gamba. Ludwig Masters Publications.

Intonation
"20 Ways to Get Your String Orchestra to Play in Tune," by Michael Alexander (2012). https://www.tmea.org/assets/pdf/southwestern_musician/20WaystoTune_Sept2012.pdf

"Teaching Tuning to the String Orchestra: Classroom Procedures for Beginning to Advanced Students," by Michael Alexander (2008). *American String Teacher*, 58(4): 20–26.

Set-Up and Playing Fundamentals
"Fourth Finger First: Why the Order of Finger Introduction Matters in Beginning String Instruction," by Sandy Goldie (2015). *American String Teacher* 65(2): 34–37.

"The Teaching of Action in String Playing," by Paul Rolland. http://www.paulrolland.net

TONE AND EXPRESSION

"Basics and Methods of Violin Playing," by Ivan Galamian. http://www.
soz-etc.com/musik/Galamian_basics-and-methods-of-violin-playing-
ENGL.html

"Mimi Zweig String Pedagogy" by Mimi Zweig. www.StringPedagogy.
com

"An Understandable Approach to Musical Expression" by Kenneth
Laudermilch (2000). Meredith Music Publications.

REPERTOIRE

"Teaching Music Through Performance in Orchestra" by Michael Allen,
Lou Bergonzi, Jacquelyn Dillon-Krass, Robert Gillespie, James
Kjelland, Dorothy Straub. Compiled and edited by David Littrell
(2008). GIA Publications

"Violin Repertoire List" by Mimi Zweig. https://music.indiana.edu
/precollege/year-round/strings/repertoire.shtml

RECRUITING/COMMUNITY BUILDING

"An Innovative Idea for Building Community and Program-Wide Support
through Creative Programming of a Spring Concert Grand Finale
Tradition," by Sandy Goldie. From *The Conductors Companion: 100
Rehearsal Techniques, Imaginative Ideas, Quotes and Facts*, compiled and edited by Gary Stith (2017). Meredith Music Publications.

"Investigating High School Band Recruitment Procedures Using
Educational Marketing Principles," by K.M. Kerstetter (2011).
Journal of Band Research, 46(2), 1–17, 59.

"Marketing Orchestra: Curbing Elementary String Attrition," by Angela
Ammerman and Brian Wuttke (2014). *American String Teachers
Journal, 64*, 22–25.

"Marketing Your Music Program: From Traditional Branding to Digital
Promotion." By Sean Dennison Smith. (2018). Meredith Music
Publications.

"Music and Social Bonding: 'Self-other' Merging and Neurohormonal
Mechanisms," by Tarr, Launay, and Dunbar (2014). *Frontiers in
Psychology*, 5.

INSTRUCTION, MANAGEMENT, SUPPORT

"A Sound-to-Symbol Approach to Learning Music," by Joyce Jordan-DeCarbo (1997). *Music Educators Journal 84*(2): 34–37, 54. (Based on Pestalozzi Principals)

Circling Around: The Violin Virtuosi. Documentary directed by Hideki Isoda. NPR. WTIU (Television station : Bloomington, Ind.), & RIAX Productions (2006). Bloomington, Ind.: Indiana University, Jacobs School of Music/WTIU.

School Orchestra and String Teachers Facebook Group. https://www.facebook.com/groups/OrchestraTeachers/

"String Instruments: Purchasing, Maintenance, Troubleshooting and More." by Sandy Goldie (2017). Meredith Music Publications.

About the Author

Sandy Goldie teaches undergraduate and graduate music education courses at Virginia Commonwealth University in Richmond, Virginia, where she is the string music education specialist and assistant professor of music education. Before moving to Richmond, Dr. Goldie taught string music education courses at the University of Florida, where she completed her PhD and was awarded the David Wilmot Prize for Excellence in Music Education. She received her master's degree in music education from the University of Georgia and her bachelor's degree in instrumental music education and performance from the University of South Carolina.

Dr. Goldie has presented her music education research and pedagogy ideas at state, national, and international conferences, including the International Society for Assessment in Music Education, National Association for Music Education, American String Teachers Association, The Midwest Clinic, Society for Music Teacher Education, and State Music Education Association Conferences in Texas, Florida, Georgia, South Carolina, and Virginia. She has worked to promote music education at the local, state, and national levels through leadership positions in professional organizations such as the American String Teachers Association (former state president of the South Carolina Chapter, current president-elect of the Virginia chapter, and chair of the college committee), South Carolina Music Educators Association (former executive board member of the orchestra division), Virginia Music Educators Association (state collegiate advisor working with NAfME chapters across the state of Virginia), American Viola Society (president-elect of South Carolina chapter and executive board member of the Virginia chapter). Dr. Goldie also serves on local arts advisory councils and works with area schools who serve disadvantaged and at-risk students to help provide access to string instruments and instruction.

Dr. Goldie is an active conductor/clinician, professional performer (violist), and advocate for music education. She enjoys working with young musicians throughout the United States and has conducted many honors groups, all-region orchestras, district clinics, youth orchestras, as well as the 2009 South Carolina All-State Orchestra. She has enjoyed working with students of all ages in the public schools as an orchestra teacher for fourteen years. Her school orchestras have consistently received superior ratings each year at state performance festivals in South Carolina, Georgia, and throughout the United States and abroad, performing in places including Hawaii (1st Place High School Orchestra Division), Italy (2007 tour of Rome, Venice, Cremona and Florence), Orlando, Williamsburg, Myrtle Beach, Atlanta, and New York. Her orchestras have also routinely performed in local nursing homes and elementary schools in order to share the joy of music and music education with others in the community. She has performed professionally with symphonies in South Carolina, North Carolina, and Georgia (South Carolina Philharmonic, Charleston Symphony, Charlotte Philharmonic, Symphony Orchestra Augusta, and others). Today, her greatest loves are her family, her dog (Murray), her new cat (Charlie), and the joy of sharing the excitement of great music teaching and performing with her students and fellow teachers.